# Deadliest Spiders

### Kris Hirschmann

San Diego, CA

© 2017 ReferencePoint Press, Inc.
Printed in the United States

**For more information, contact:**
ReferencePoint Press, Inc.
PO Box 27779
San Diego, CA 92198
www. ReferencePointPress.com

LIBRARY OF CONGRESS CATALOGING-IN-PUBLICATION DATA

Names: Hirschmann, Kris, 1967- , author.
Title: Deadliest spiders / by Kris Hirschmann.
Description: San Diego, CA : ReferencePoint Press, 2017. | Series: Deadliest predators | Includes bibliographical references and index. | Audience: Grades 9 to 12.
Identifiers: LCCN 2016020674 (print) | LCCN 2016023540 (ebook) | ISBN 9781682820582 (hardback) | ISBN 9781682820599 (eBook)
Subjects: LCSH: Poisonous spiders--Juvenile literature.
Classification: LCC QL458.4 .H57 2017 (print) | LCC QL458.4 (ebook) | DDC 595.4/4165--dc23
LC record available at https://lccn.loc.gov/2016020674

# Contents

# Fodder for Phobias

Spiders are among the most common creatures on Earth. Nearly forty-six thousand species had been discovered by the end of 2015, and new species are continuing to be named as scientific study moves into previously unexplored areas of the planet. It is fair to assume that many thousands of spider species remain to be found and named.

The world's known spiders are currently divided among about 114 families, although this number varies slightly according to the source. All spiders in all families have venom, which is a type of modified saliva that contains toxins. The toxins vary from spider to spider. They generally have a strong effect on the spider's usual prey but little to no effect on other creatures.

Humans fall under the latter category. Spiders do not naturally hunt or kill people. Over millions of years their venom has evolved to quickly kill insects, lizards, arthropods, or whatever prey the specific type of spider hunts. When it comes to humans, though, most spiders are completely harmless.

## A Few Exceptions

But there are exceptions to this rule. A few spider families possess venom that does, through some accident of evolution, have a strong effect on humans. Scientists refer to these arachnids as being "medically important." Widow, recluse, funnel-web, and banana spiders are proven and highly feared human killers. Mouse spiders and Old World tarantulas are not known to have killed—yet—but their painful bites and powerful venom can and do make people critically ill.

It might be said that these few dangerous arachnids have spoiled things for the rest, at least from a human viewpoint. Studies show that on average, people fear spiders more than anything else in the world, including heights, the dark, public speaking, or anything else that might come to mind. There is even a name for the irrational fear of spiders: arachnophobia. People who suffer from arachnophobia arrange their whole lives in a way that avoids spiders. Some arachnophobes are too fearful to even look at a picture of a spider or to see one on television.

Most people are not quite this extreme in their feelings. But apart from serious enthusiasts and scientists, few people really like spiders. A big eight-legged arachnid on a wall or, worse, on a person's bare foot is virtually guaranteed to elicit squeals and shudders.

## Spider Benefits

These squeals and shudders, however, should be accompanied by a nod of thanks. People benefit from spiders every day in a multitude of ways.

Perhaps the biggest spider benefit is the reduction of the insect population. Although insects are not the spider's only prey, they are the main one. Spiders trap vast quantities of flying and crawling bugs in their webs and through other hunting methods. By doing so, they play a huge role in keeping insects under control. This in turn has many benefits for people. Fewer disease-carrying mosquitoes in an area, for instance, might reduce human

*A bite from a tarantula, like the one pictured here, is highly venomous and thus dangerous but probably not deadly to humans. The same cannot be said for a small group of other spiders, whose bites can cause serious illness and death.*

malaria rates. Fewer crop-eating larvae might make farms healthier and increase the supply of vital foods across an entire region.

Spiders have medical benefits too, although this is a fairly new field and much is still to be discovered. Scientists are currently studying spider venom to see if it can be used in medicines for arthritis, pain control, and reversing the effects of stroke. Since many spider venoms contain neurotoxins, which are substances that affect the nervous system, researchers also hope to find uses in nerve- and brain-related disorders.

Yet another benefit may come from spider silk. This remarkable substance is roughly six times stronger than a steel strand of the same width. It is currently used inside some optical instruments, such as laboratory telescopes. Harvesting spider silk is not easy, so large-scale uses may be more challenging to develop, but other small-scale applications are sure to be found over time.

## Worthy of Respect

These benefits probably will not turn a spider-fearing person into a spider lover—and there may be a biological reason for that. Some scientists suggest that a fear of spiders is actually built into the human gene pool. They think that the earliest humans evolved in areas where venomous spiders were common. People who feared these creatures would avoid them and stay alive to pass their genes to the next generation of humans. Although the danger is now mostly gone, the fear remains as a permanent part of human DNA.

But like most fears, this one can be reduced through knowledge. People who learn more about spiders will come to understand that these creatures are both fascinating and largely harmless. The few that are dangerous can be easily recognized—and avoided. Spiders may not be the monsters that some people make them out to be, but they deserve a healthy level of respect nonetheless.

# Chapter 1

# Black Widow

The genus *Latrodectus* contains thirty-one spider species that, as a group, are among the most feared creatures on Earth. The terrifying lineup includes the button spiders of Africa, the redback of Australia, the katipo of New Zealand, and many widow spiders found around the world.

All *Latrodectus* species are venomous. However, the southern black widow of North America stands out from the crowd in terms of its deadly potential. Usually called the black widow, this creature is highly venomous and widespread. It is common in human-inhabited areas and comes into frequent contact with people. Vicious, painful bites—and sometimes deaths—are the unfortunate result.

## Body Basics

The female black widow is one of the world's most recognized spiders thanks to its dramatic body coloring. Like all arachnids, this creature has an exoskeleton, which is a hard external shell that supports and protects the body's soft interior. The exoskeleton of the female black widow is an inky, shiny black in most places. The underside bears a blood-red marking in the shape of an hourglass.

Male and juvenile black widows look quite different from adult females. Males are black in most places but have orange-brown segments on their legs. Their abdomens bear red and white stripes instead of the classic hourglass mark. Juvenile black widows are orange, brown, and white and develop their adult coloring as they grow.

*The female southern black widow spider is identifiable by the telltale red hourglass on its abdomen. This dramatic coloring makes the black widow one of the world's most recognized spiders.*

Female and male black widows are different in their size and shape too. Including the legs, females are about 1.5 inches (4 cm) long, with a 0.4 inch (1 cm) central body. Like all spiders, this creature's body is divided into two segments. The abdomen, which contains the gut, heart, reproductive glands, and silk-making glands, is rounded and very large in relation to the cephalothorax (head and trunk). The abdomen swells even larger when the spider is carrying eggs. Males are generally one-third to one-half the size of females, with elongated instead of rounded abdomens.

A close-up look reveals other features. The black widow's eight long, slender legs are attached to the cephalothorax. They have seven jointed segments and are tipped with sharp claws. The rear claws are covered with bristles and are known as comb feet—a trait shared by all of the spiders in the black widow's family. At the back end of the spider's abdomen are six spinnerets that make silk. At the front end are two pedipalps, or feelers, that the spider uses to touch, taste, and smell objects as well as to move food to the mouth. Between the pedipalps are the two chelicerae, or jaws, that contain the spider's fangs.

## Range and Habitat

North America is home to several black widow species. The most dangerous is the southern black widow, which is found mostly in the southeastern United States. It is common throughout the area bounded by Texas to the west, Ohio to the north, and Florida to the south. It is sometimes found outside this range, particularly in the deserts of the American Southwest, and it is also spotted occasionally in California and southeastern Canada.

# THE BLACK WIDOW AT A GLANCE

- **Scientific name:** *Latrodectus mactans*
- **Scientific family:** Theridiidae
- **Range:** Southeastern United States, Hawaii, Dominican Republic
- **Habitat:** Widespread, including grasslands, tropical rain forests, and forests
- **Size (including legs):** 1.5 inches (4 cm)
- **Diet:** Insects, wood lice, centipedes, millipedes, other spiders
- **Life span:** Up to three years
- **Key features:** Shiny black body with red hourglass-shaped mark
- **Deadly because:** Has highly toxic venom

Additionally, southern black widows are well established in the Hawaiian Islands and the Dominican Republic.

Other black widow species are closely related to the southern black widow, but their primary ranges are different. Their looks also vary slightly. In particular, the bold hourglass marking is less pronounced or missing in other North American species.

Within their home range, black widows are found in many different habitats. They will happily inhabit woodlands, tropical rain forests, grasslands, and deserts. All they really need is a dark, dry, sheltered area, such as a woodpile, a crack-filled rocky hillside, an abandoned animal burrow, or the spreading branches of low-growing plants. Any natural crevice makes a good shelter for a black widow.

The same applies to nooks and crannies that occur around human homes. Black widows do not mind living near people and will settle among firewood, under the rims of trash can lids, inside storage sheds, under dusty porches, and anywhere else they can find a quiet resting spot. If people leave clothing or shoes outside overnight, black widows may even crawl into these tempting spots and get to work building a home.

*After catching a grasshopper in her web, a black widow wraps it in her sticky silk and then sinks her fangs into the body. The fangs deliver a fast-acting, paralyzing dose of venom.*

# The Black Widow at Home

For black widows, this process involves spinning a web. The web is made of silk that the spider makes with its spinnerets. The spinnerets squirt out liquid proteins that harden on contact with the air. The spider pulls this protein string out of its body, longer and longer, to produce a tough strand that will become part of its web.

Black widows do not spin organized webs. At first glance, their nests look like a tangled mass of coarse lines running every which way. Careful examination, though, shows that the black widow's messy home has three distinct areas. At the top are supporting threads that attach the web to an object. Below the supporting threads is a region of tangled threads. At the very bottom are the vertical trap threads, which are strung tightly and stuck to the ground with blobs of gooey material.

At the side of the web is a retreat zone where the black widow spends most of its time. The spider will leave its retreat to repair the web, when necessary, or to gather food. But it does these things as little as possible—and it almost never ventures away from the web entirely. Black widows are clumsy and slow away from their webs. To keep themselves safe, they stay in their retreats and hang, head down, waiting for food to approach.

# On the Hunt

Food might be many different things for a black widow. These spiders eat just about anything they can catch, including insects, wood lice, millipedes, centipedes, and other spiders.

The meal begins when one of these creatures bumbles into the black widow's trap lines. The lines break away from the ground below with huge force. The sticky anchoring blobs slam into the intruder's body as they rocket toward the main part of the web. The unsuspecting prey is instantly glued to the strand and yanked upward—right into the heart of the black widow's lair.

Even though it has eight eyes, the black widow does not see this happen. Its eyesight is very poor. However, its sense of touch is excellent—and the spider feels every little vibration as its deadly trap is sprung. The black widow rushes out of its retreat toward the struggling prey. It begins extruding silk and uses its comb feet to fling this silk around and around the prey. Before long the prey is completely wrapped up in sticky silk and unable to move.

At this point the spider moves in for the kill. It opens its jaws wide and extends its fangs, which are hollow, like hypodermic needles. It plunges the fangs into the prey's body and delivers a dose of venom that quickly paralyzes the victim. The spider waits until its prey is completely frozen, then drags it back to the retreat to be eaten.

The meal process is messy and gruesome but effective. The black widow uses sharp, pinching teeth to tear a wound in the prey and then vomits a digestive liquid into the wound. The liquid digests the prey's flesh, turning it into watery mush. The black widow sucks up this fluid using a straw-shaped mouthpart. It repeats this process over and over, digesting and eating a little bit of the prey at a time, until its hunger is satisfied.

## The Danger to Humans

A human is much too big for a black widow to eat in this manner. A black widow can, however, bite a person. If it does, the results can be life threatening or even, in the most extreme circumstances, fatal.

# A MURDEROUS MATE

Black widows get their common nickname from their mating behavior. A widow is a female whose husband has died—and female black widows sometimes kill and eat their mates after mating has occurred.

The females of some widow species are more likely to engage in this practice than others. The redback of Australia is particularly prone to eating its mate. Most other species, however, including the southern black widow, are just as likely to go their separate ways without any bloodshed.

The outcome of a mating encounter seems to depend mostly on the surroundings. If there are plenty of easy escape routes, the male will probably survive. If the male is trapped in the female's presence, though, he will probably end up becoming a meal. This does not have anything to do with the mating process; it is a simple matter of hunger. After all, the female needs to eat—and any smaller creature that ventures too close, including a mate, puts itself into deadly peril.

Substances called neurotoxins are responsible for this effect, which is called latrodectism. The black widow's neurotoxins work by attacking the victim's nerve endings. In response, the nerves pump chemicals into the system that make many parts of the body, particularly the muscles, function abnormally. Extreme, unrelenting cramps of the abdomen and other major muscle groups, including the heart, may occur. The victim will also experience extreme sweating, high blood pressure, nausea, and vomiting. These symptoms can progress to shock, coma, and eventually to death.

A reporter named Jackson Landers experienced many of these symptoms when he was bitten by a black widow near his home in Virginia. In a 2013 article, Landers described the progression of his symptoms. When bitten, he recalls, "I felt a stinging sensation. . . . Then the pain increased to about that of a wasp's sting." Soon, he says, "I felt a warmth in my abdomen. This turned into pressure, which became a painful cramping." At this point, Landers headed to the hospital. Before long, he says, "The pain had crept into my lower chest, sending out waves of muscle spasms. . . . My biceps cramped. I shivered and twitched uncontrollably."[1]

*A man displays a wound caused by the bite of a black widow spider. Although black widow spider bites are not usually fatal to humans, the spider's usual prey rarely escape death.*

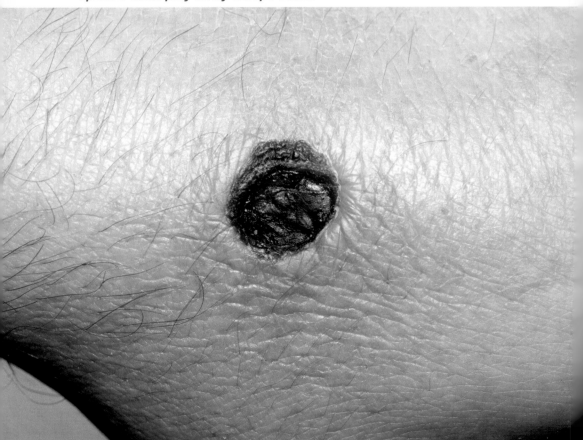

Landers received treatment for his symptoms and was fine within a few days, with no lingering effects from his black widow encounter. This is the case for most people who are bitten by black widows. In 2014, the most recent year for which statistics are available, a reported 1,692 black widow bites in the United States did not lead to a single death. In countries where health care is less available, outcomes are worse—but not much. Although estimates vary, most experts place the risk of death from untreated latrodectism at less than 1 percent.

## An Unexpected Appearance

A low risk, however, is not the same as no risk. Caution is well advised for anyone who lives in areas where black widows are likely to make their homes. People who live in rural areas, particularly, should always wear gloves when reaching into nooks and crannies. They should also check their shoes—as Jackson Landers knows all too well. Landers's life-threatening bite was delivered by a black widow that had stowed away in water shoes sitting on an open-air front porch.

Even people in urban areas, where spiders are less common, may encounter black widows thanks to these arachnids' habit of spinning webs on growing crops. Store-bought grapes are the most common source of unexpected urban black widow encounters—one of which sent a Vermont woman to the hospital in May 2015.

The good news is that black widows are not aggressive and would rather not attack people. They only bite if they are trapped and scared. If a black widow does show up in a shopper's bag, it will scuttle away if possible. By letting these spiders do what comes naturally, people can avoid being bitten and keep themselves safe.

# Chapter 2

# Brazilian Wandering Spider

The heart of Brazil's Amazon rain forest is home to one of the planet's deadliest spiders. Called the Brazilian wandering spider or sometimes the banana or armed spider, this arachnid is big, hairy, and potentially deadly to any human unlucky enough to cross its path.

Brazilian wandering spiders are members of the *Phoneutria* genus, which contains eight species. All eight species are native to South America. All are venomous and can deliver painful bites. Even among this dangerous group, though, the Brazilian wandering spider stands out due to its venom's wicked potency. This arachnid has all the tools it needs to subdue prey in its jungle home.

## Body Basics

The Brazilian wandering spider is a large arachnid. Individuals can measure up to 7 inches (18 cm) across, including the legs. As is true in many spider species, females tend to be larger than males.

The Brazilian wandering spider is not just big; it is sturdy too. This creature has a large, rounded, bulbous abdomen attached to a cephalothorax of a similar size. Eight long legs protrude from the cephalothorax in pairs. The first and fourth pairs of legs are the longest, and the second and third pairs are smaller. Each leg has either four or five joints that work like human elbows to give the spider a wide range of movement.

The coloration of the Brazilian wandering spider is dramatic. The dominant color is tan. The legs match this color where they meet the body but darken along their length until they reach a deep black at their clawed ends. The leg joints, in contrast, are a vivid yellow that stands out clearly from the background shade. The spider's chelicerae, too, stand out; they are covered with a coat of fine crimson hairs that can be displayed or hidden, as the spider chooses.

Like the chelicerae, the rest of the Brazilian wandering spider's body is also hairy. The hairs give the spider a fuzzy appearance, as if it is sporting beard stubble of one or two days' growth all over. The hairs are not there to keep the spider warm, as they might be in a mammal; the Brazilian wandering spider is cold-blooded and gets its body heat from the environment. Instead, the tiny hairs function as sensory receptors, collecting touch information and sending it to the spider's brain. The hairs are so sensitive that they can pick up air vibrations from flying insects, alerting the spider that prey is nearby.

The eyes provide some information about the spider's environment as well. The Brazilian wandering spider has eight eyes, arranged in three rows at the front of the head. The top row contains two large, dark eyes that are the most sensitive of the set. The second row contains four small eyes, and the third row has two more. By combining the visual information from these organs, along with the touch data from its sensory hairs, the spider keeps track of its surroundings.

*The Brazilian wandering spider (pictured), also known as the banana spider, is among the world's deadliest. The spider gets its name from its habit of moving from place to place.*

## Home and Habits

These surroundings are typically green, lush, and visually chaotic. The Brazilian wandering spider is found mostly in the deep Amazon rain forest, which explodes with plant and animal life of all types. The spider is just one small member of this vibrant community. The Brazilian wandering spider has also been reported in nearby parts of South and Central America, but it is much less common in these areas.

Within its rain forest home, the Brazilian wandering spider is a ground dweller and a nomad. It does not build a web or stick to a specific lair or resting spot day after day, as many spiders do. Instead, it wanders from place to place, which is how this arachnid got its name. It keeps to itself as it travels. These creatures are aggressive and territorial and do not live with or near other wandering spiders.

Brazilian wandering spiders are nocturnal. This means they are most active during the night. They take shelter under logs, in crevices, inside hanging plants, or in other dark, damp places during the daytime hours. As night approaches, the spiders become active and begin to stir—and when full darkness falls, they emerge from their hiding places. They are ready to go on the hunt.

## On the Hunt

Many spiders sit and wait for prey to come to them. But for Brazilian wandering spiders, hunting is a busy and active process. These creatures roam the jungle floor in the dark of night, creeping on their long legs through vegetation in search of prey. Quiet and stealthy, they keep their senses alert for signs of possible prey. The spider's menu might include large insects such as katydids, crickets, and mantids along with larger animals such as tree frogs and lizards. Even small mammals, such as mice, may become a meal for this deadly hunter.

When a Brazilian wandering spider senses a vulnerable animal nearby, it prepares to attack. It moves as close as possible to the creature—and then it pounces. This arachnid is fast and strong, and it seizes the prey with its legs before the animal realizes the deadly peril it is in. The Brazilian wandering spider then swings its hollow fangs outward, extending them like two pinchers that come together like a crab's claws, and plunges them into the prey's flesh. It injects a killing dose of venom—a small dose for a small creature and a larger dose for a bigger one—and then waits.

It does not have to wait long. The trapped prey struggles mightily for a short time as the spider's venom surges through its body. Within about fifteen seconds

*The Brazilian wandering spider has eight eyes that enable it to see in the dark. These, along with body hairs that function as sensory receptors, provide information about the movements of potential prey and make the spider a formidable predator.*

# THE BRAZILIAN WANDERING SPIDER AT A GLANCE

- **Scientific name:** *Phoneutria fera*
- **Scientific family:** Ctenidae
- **Range:** Brazilian Amazon region
- **Habitat:** Tropical rain forests
- **Size (including legs):** Up to 7 inches (18 cm)
- **Diet:** Insects, small lizards, mice
- **Life span:** Up to two years
- **Key features:** Hairy, red jaws
- **Deadly because:** Most potent venom of any spider

the prey starts to weaken as its nervous system fails. It becomes more and more sluggish until it stops moving completely, as little as a minute after being bitten.

The spider is now ready to enjoy its dinner. Like other spiders, it vomits digestive fluids to dissolve the prey's soft parts into a puddle of nutritious goop. It sucks the soupy mess into its stomach. The entire digestion process has been completed outside of the body, so the spider's system can immediately absorb the nutrients from the meal.

## Deadly Venom

The fast-acting venom of the Brazilian wandering spider is a big part of this arachnid's hunting success. The venom contains more than 150 different proteins, including several potent neurotoxins that make the bite victim's bodily functions go haywire. Although there are several ways to measure the toxicity of venom, and different standards apply to different spiders, scientists widely agree that the Brazilian wandering spider is the world's most venomous arachnid.

The Brazilian wandering spider holds this title in part because of its size. All venomous spiders have venom glands inside their bodies where they store their poison. A small spider can only store a little bit of venom. A very large spider, on the other hand, has room to store a great deal of liquid in its venom glands. The Brazilian wandering spider combines lots of storage space with a particularly potent cocktail of toxins, making it a potentially lethal double threat.

A person who is bitten by this spider will get a first-hand demonstration of this fact. Immediately after being bitten, the victim will feel intense pain and burning at the bite site as nerve endings under the skin react to the spider's venom. As the poison spreads farther into the body, the person may experience blurred vision, heavy sweating, tremors, and vomiting. Blood pressure may rise or drop. In extreme cases, the victim may lose muscle control and develop severe breathing problems. If these symptoms are not treated, the bite victim will die from paralysis and respiratory failure.

## Human Encounters

An incident from the 1960s illustrates this danger. Two children were sleeping in the same bed in a house in rural Brazil when a wandering spider entered the room. The creature climbed into the bed and bit both children, who subsequently died. The incident was reported by

*The wandering spider preys on large insects and small animals such as tree frogs, lizards, and even mice. Here, a spider consumes a tree frog that it has killed with its venomous bite.*

a local naturalist after the spider was brought to him for identification.

This story is not the only example. Other deaths have been caused by the Brazilian wandering spider's bite, although not many; scientific literature has only confirmed 10 to 14 cases in total. A study published in 2000, in fact,

# BANANA SPIDERS?

Brazilian wandering spiders have a well-known reputation for hiding in banana bunches. This is why they are often called banana spiders. A quick online search for news stories on this topic turns up accounts from people around the world who claim to have found these deadly creatures in their fruit.

But were these spiders really *Phoneutria fera (P. fera)*, the lethal Brazilian species? Experts think it is unlikely in most cases. They point out that many *Phoneutria* species look similar to one another and may be easily confused by amateur naturalists. They also make the excellent point that bananas are not grown in the deep Amazon rain forest where the Brazilian spiders mostly roam. So although big, hairy spiders certainly do turn up in store-bought bananas, they are probably not the Brazilian wandering variety.

That fact might not soothe people who encounter enormous eight-legged hitchhikers in their kitchens. All *Phoneutria* species are venomous, and all will bite when threatened. But as long as people avoid *P. fera*, they should survive to enjoy their bananas in peace and good health.

suggested that bites are much more common than serious outcomes. Out of 422 known cases, only 9 percent of patients experienced moderate to severe symptoms, and only one patient—a three-year-old child—died as a result.

One reason for this low number of fatalities is probably the fact that the Brazilian wandering spider can choose how much venom to inject into a victim. When it bites a human in self-defense, it often delivers a dry (venomless) bite or injects just a small dose of toxins. Still, the bite is not pleasant, as one British victim recalls. "It felt like a rose thorn. It was extremely painful," says Matthew Stevens, who was bitten in 2005 but recovered fully from the experience. "I was never scared of spiders before, but I certainly am now."[2]

## Stay Away

If a person does happen to encounter a Brazilian wandering spider, he or she will be given ample opportunity to back off. The frightened arachnid mounts an impressive threat display that looks aggressive but is actually designed to scare threatening creatures—such as large, scary humans—into leaving the spider alone.

In the threat display, the Brazilian wandering spider turns to face the perceived attacker. It raises its first two pairs of legs off the ground and locks the joints, holding the legs straight up in the air to expose the vivid colors underneath. At the same time, it spreads its chelicerae and exposes the bright red hairs that line the jaws. It also raises its pedipalps above its head, like a boxer's ready-to-punch fists. The spider holds this position until the threat retreats. If the human or other threat ignores the spider's warning and comes closer, the spider is likely to leap forward and bite.

The Brazilian wandering spider uses this technique mostly to discourage its natural predators, which include rodents, birds, and insects called tarantula hawks. The display certainly works equally well on humans though, most of whom are a little bit squeamish about giant spiders to begin with. The threat display is just one more incentive—and a powerful one, at that—to leave this deadly predator alone.

# Chapter 3

# Chilean Recluse

Many people in the English-speaking world know about the brown recluse, a highly venomous spider native to the central region of the United States. Fewer people know that the brown recluse has a similar but much more dangerous relative living south of the border. Native to South America, the lethal Chilean recluse poses a deadly danger wherever it appears.

The Chilean recluse is a member of the *Loxosceles* genus, which includes about one hundred recluse species worldwide. All of these spiders are venomous to some degree. Most recluses, however, lack the venom strength or quantity to be dangerous to people. But the Chilean recluse has plenty of both. When this spider bites, the effects are painful at best and, in some cases, may even be fatal.

## Body Basics

The Chilean recluse is on the large side for the recluse family. A typical specimen measures about 1.25 inches (3.2 cm) across (including the legs). Some individuals grow even larger, up to more than 1.5 inches (3.8 cm) across.

The central body of this spider is divided into two distinct parts. The abdomen is rounded in the female and elongated in the male and is a solid dark brown color. The cephalothorax is smaller than the abdomen. Its background color is a yellowish brown, with a darker brown violin-shaped mark running from front to back. Many recluse spiders have this type of marking. For this reason, recluses are nicknamed fiddlebacks in many parts of the world.

*The Chilean recluse spider (pictured) is related to the brown recluse that is native to the central United States. Its bite is destructive and sometimes deadly to humans.*

The spider's eight jointed legs are attached to the sides of the cephalothorax. The legs are long and slender, with thicker hairy segments near the body. The central parts of the legs are smooth, yellowish, and straight. The two end segments of each leg are thinner, hairier, and darker in color than the middle parts.

Protruding straight out from the front of the cephalothorax are two pedipalps. In the Chilean recluse, these appendages are long and very obvious. Between the pedipalps are the thick, hair-covered chelicerae, which house the spider's venomous fangs.

At first glance, the Chilean recluse seems to have three round, jet-black eyes staring out from its face. Yet a closer look shows that there are actually three pairs of eyes. Since most spiders have eight eyes instead of six, this is a distinguishing feature of all recluse spiders.

## Range and Habitat

As its name suggests, the Chilean recluse is most common in the South American nation of Chile. It is also found in neighboring countries, including Peru, Ecuador, Argentina, Uruguay, and southern and eastern Brazil. A few isolated populations of Chilean recluses occur in Central America, but the spider is not widespread in this area.

Within its home range, the Chilean recluse prefers to settle in dry, warm, dark places. In the wild, it seeks out cracks and crevices within rotting tree bark, beneath fallen logs, and under rocks. Whenever it can, though, this spider prefers to live near human habitations, where there tend to be fewer predators and better hiding spots. The Chilean recluse happily takes shelter under building eaves, inside sheds, in basements and garages, inside

# THE CHILEAN RECLUSE AT A GLANCE

- **Scientific name:** *Loxosceles laeta*
- **Scientific family:** Sicariidae
- **Range:** Parts of South America
- **Habitat:** Around human homes in temperate areas
- **Size (including legs):** About 1.25 inches (3.2 cm)
- **Diet:** Insects, arthropods
- **Life span:** Two years
- **Key features:** Violin-shaped mark on back
- **Deadly because:** Strong venom and proximity to people

boxes, and anywhere else it will remain hidden and undisturbed.

Scientific studies have shown that the Chilean recluse prefers vertical cracks to horizontal ones. This tendency leads the spider to establish itself in out-of-the-way corners inside human homes. Because of this habit, the Chilean recluse is commonly called *araña de rincón*, which means "corner spider" in Spanish.

Despite the fact that the Chilean recluse often lives among people, it is very shy and reclusive—a behavior that is common to all recluse spiders and which gives this group its name. A home can be infested with hundreds of these spiders without the human residents suspecting a thing. In fact, Chilean recluses tend to congregate in large numbers, and it is unusual for just one of these spiders to live on its own. If a person spies one

Chilean recluse skittering across the floor of a house, it is extremely likely that more spiders—potentially *many more spiders*—are lurking nearby.

There is a good reason why Chilean recluses are so seldom seen. These arachnids hide themselves away during the daytime hours, when they are more likely to be spotted by predators or humans. They rest comfortably in their tangled, messy webs while they wait for darkness to fall.

## On the Hunt

When night arrives, the Chilean recluse springs into action. It leaves its web, which is not designed to be a hunting tool, as it is for many spiders. Instead, the Chilean recluse is an active hunter that is fast, agile, and capable of running down its prey. Common targets include cockroaches, crickets, and other crawling creatures. The Chilean recluse will also eat other spiders and small arthropods, if it gets the chance. It is equally happy to scavenge its meals and will consume any dead creatures it finds lying around.

When taking live prey, the Chilean recluse uses its venom as a powerful killing tool. The spider chases and pounces on the prey, then delivers a swift bite with its small but needle-sharp fangs. It pumps venom into the prey's body, then backs off and waits for the toxins to take effect.

The process does not take long. The venom spreads quickly through the victim's system and begins breaking down the internal organs and flesh. The poisoned creature grows weaker and weaker as its vital parts dissolve. It soon dies—and only then does the Chilean recluse move in for its meal. The hungry spider sucks down its predigested prey like a gory smoothie in a perfect insect-shaped cup.

## Nasty Venom

Recluse venom gets its toxicity from a cocktail of proteins. The most important protein is a substance called sphyingomyelinase D (SMD). All recluse spiders have this protein, which otherwise exists only in a few types of bacteria. Unlike the neurotoxins of many other spiders, which work to disable the nervous system, SMD attacks and kills living cells. In scientific language, it is called a dermonecrotizing (skin-killing) agent.

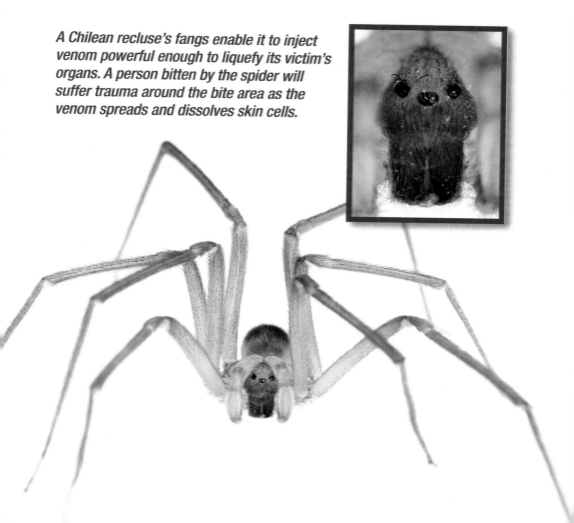

*A Chilean recluse's fangs enable it to inject venom powerful enough to liquefy its victim's organs. A person bitten by the spider will suffer trauma around the bite area as the venom spreads and dissolves skin cells.*

# WORLD TRAVELERS

All types of recluse spiders will crawl into dark boxes, pallets, and other shipping materials to rest during the daytime hours. These arachnids are also able to live for long periods without food or water. For both of these reasons, recluses sometimes hitchhike from their home areas to faraway places, where they may establish new populations.

This is true of the Chilean recluse, which is now found in several places outside its natural range. Populations of this spider exist today in Canada; Massachusetts; Florida; and Los Angeles, California. Perhaps the best-known foreign population lives in the Natural History Museum in Helsinki, Finland. Local schools often take field trips to this museum. The students' parents must sign permission slips explaining the potential danger.

Luckily, no deaths have occurred in this museum or in any of the Chilean recluse's other foreign homes. The foreign populations also do not seem to be spreading. This spider's reclusive nature keeps it well hidden and confined to one place—and that is good news for all nearby humans.

The effects of a Chilean recluse's bite illustrate this term in a shockingly gruesome fashion. When first bitten, a person feels very little pain—perhaps just a tiny prick. Over the course of the next two to eight hours, however, a sharp pain develops at the bite site, followed by a burning sensation. The skin reddens, swells, and blisters as the cells below the surface start to dissolve.

Over the next few days the trauma around the bite worsens. The damaged area darkens to a deep purple and spreads outward as the venom reaches and attacks more and more flesh. The skin's upper layer sloughs off to reveal an open, oozing crater full of pus and black, dead material. The size of the crater depends on the severity of the bite. Mild bites may result in small lesions. Bad ones can cause horrifying wounds as much as 16 inches (41 cm) across.

The damage spreads for several days to a week, depending on the amount of venom originally injected. After this acute phase, the lesion stops growing—but the victim's suffering is far from over. A small lesion will take six to eight weeks to heal fully and will leave a permanent scar. Larger lesions, on the other hand, have lasted for years in the most extreme cases—and some are so severe that they will never heal. Doctors must amputate the patient's limb to resolve the problem.

## From Bad to Worse

All of these effects together are called cutaneous loxoscelism. The word *cutaneous* means "of the skin." It means that the recluse venom stays within the skin and does not spread deeper into the victim's body. Although patients with cutaneous loxoscelism experience many unpleasant symptoms, as described above, they are not likely to die as a result of their encounter with the Chilean recluse.

In a small percentage of cases, however, the recluse venom spreads beyond the skin into the patient's circulatory system, where it is able to travel throughout the body. This causes a more severe condition called viscerocutaneous loxoscelism. The first sign of this spread is the onset of body-wide symptoms, including itching, chills, fever, nausea, and sweating. These symptoms reflect the battle raging inside the body, where the patient's red blood cells are under attack from the recluse's venom. These cells die in droves. The kidneys, which work to remove waste from the bloodstream, cannot keep up with the carnage, and they may fail under the pressure. Without immediate treatment, the patient will die.

Thankfully, this type of loxoscelism is much less common than the skin-only variety, and deaths from the Chilean recluse's bite are rare. A survey of 216 bite cases found that only 34 patients (15.7 percent) developed the systemic variety of the disorder. Of these, eight died, making the overall death rate for all 216 patients about 3.7 percent. And it is worth noting that this study was conducted in 1989. Since then, treatments and outcomes have improved, so the survival rate for loxoscelism victims is undoubtedly better than these numbers suggest.

## Lingering Effects

But that fact is little consolation for people who suffer the Chilean recluse's bite. A man named Jonathon Hogg recalls his experience after being bitten by a recluse spider that had snuck onto an airline flight in 2015. "The pain was like nothing I've been through in my life. By the time I got to [the] hospital my leg was bursting open, there was pus, it was black. . . . It resembled something from a horror film,"[3] he recalls. Hogg ended up spending a month in the hospital, where he endured three operations and a skin graft. Thanks to these efforts, he narrowly avoided losing his leg and his life. But the scars from his encounter will remain forever.

No one knows which type of recluse bit Hogg. But all recluse venom works in a similar way—and scientists

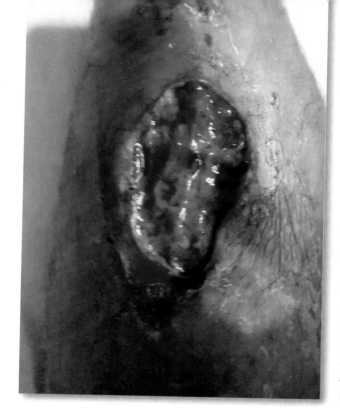

*British traveler Jonathon Hogg was bitten by a recluse spider on an airline flight in 2015, resulting in this lesion. The bite forced Hogg to spend a month in the hospital.*

know that the Chilean recluse's venom glands hold up to seven times more venom than any other species. If a less venomous type caused Hogg's devastating bite, one can only imagine what the Chilean variety could do. When it comes to deadly potential, this spider definitely deserves a spot among the worst of the worst.

# Chapter 4

# Sydney Funnel-Web Spider

Funnel-web spiders are found around the world in warm regions. There are about forty different species that have similar body features and behaviors, including the tendency to build funnel-shaped webs—the trait that gives this family its name.

Another trait that funnel-web spiders share is their dangerous bite. All funnel-web spiders are venomous. In most species the venom is mild and has a weak effect on humans. The Sydney funnel-web spider of Australia, however, is an exception to the rule. This spider has one of the most powerful venoms in the animal kingdom. It also lives near humans and is known to be aggressive. Between these factors, the Sydney funnel-web is considered by many experts to be the world's most dangerous spider.

## Body Basics

The Sydney funnel-web spider is a fairly large species. Body length averages about 1 inch (2.5 cm) in males and 1.4 inches (3.6 cm) in females. Adding the legs to this measurement, however, increases the size considerably. A spread-out individual can easily measure 3 inches (7.6 cm) across or, in extremely rare cases, even more. The Australian Reptile Park near Sydney received a specimen measuring 4 inches (10 cm) across in February 2016. Equally enormous individuals surely still lurk, undiscovered, in the wild.

This spider has a sturdy build to go with its large size. The cephalothorax and abdomen are big and bulbous. In females, these two body parts are roughly equal in size; in males, the abdomen is significantly smaller. The

*The Sydney funnel-web spider (pictured) has dark black legs with easily visible joints. It raises its front legs (as seen here) when it takes a defensive stance.*

# THE SYDNEY FUNNEL-WEB SPIDER AT A GLANCE

- **Scientific name:** *Atrax robustus*
- **Scientific family:** Hexathelidae
- **Range:** Eastern Australia, in and around Sydney
- **Habitat:** Forests, urban areas
- **Size (including legs):** Up to 4 inches (10 cm)
- **Diet:** Crawling insects, arthropods, snails, small vertebrates
- **Life span:** About eight years
- **Key features:** Sturdy, glossy black body
- **Deadly because:** Aggressive and highly venomous

cephalothorax is hairless and colored a deep, glossy black. The spider's eight thick legs are also a deep black but are hairy in places. They protrude from the cephalothorax with the many joints clearly visible. The abdomen is covered with velvety hair and is brownish rather than black. At the rear of the abdomen are two large, visible spinnerets that the spider uses to make its silk.

At the front of the cephalothorax are two long, thick pedipalps that are so big that they look almost like another pair of legs. Between these two appendages are the huge and terrifying chelicerae, each of which is double the thickness of a leg. The chelicerae end in fangs that point straight downward rather than pinching inward, as they do in many spiders. Each fang is needle sharp and nearly .5 inches (1.3 cm) long.

# Home and Habits

The Sydney funnel-web spider is named for its home range. This spider is native to the eastern edge of Australia. It is found only within about 100 miles (160 km) of Sydney, the country's most populous city.

Within its home region, the Sydney funnel-web seeks areas of lush vegetation where humidity is high and the soil is damp. This spider is a burrower, so it stays away from places where the ground is too loose, such as on beaches, or too hard, such as in tight-packed clay. Instead, it makes its home where digging conditions are good. This means the soil is wet and hard enough to form stable tunnels but soft enough for easy excavation. The ground beneath rocks and fallen timber, within compost heaps, and underneath human homes all make good nesting places for this arachnid.

When a Sydney funnel-web finds a good spot, it starts to dig. It creates a burrow that is just wide enough for the spider to enter comfortably and anywhere from 8 to 24 inches (20 to 61 cm) deep. Within this burrow, the spider uses its spinnerets to create silk strands. It weaves these strands into a long, funnel-shaped web, somewhat like a silk stocking, that is anchored to the inner end of the burrow by long strands of tough silk. The funnel's open outer end is attached to the burrow's entrance with short, fine strands that extend outward around the hole, like a rim of eyelashes.

The Sydney funnel-web's body dries out easily in sunlight. This spider therefore spends the daylight hours resting deep within its burrow where conditions are cool and damp. It waits for the night to arrive. When darkness has fallen, the spider creeps closer to the burrow's entrance and waits for potential prey to wander nearby.

# On the Hunt

Prey for the Sydney funnel-web spider might be just about any small, crawling creature. This spider seems to have a particular love for millipedes, but it is known to eat beetles, cockroaches, insect larvae, and snails as well. It will also take a frog or a small lizard if the opportunity arises.

To find food, the Sydney funnel-web uses the outer silk strands of its web as an alert system. When small creatures accidentally bump into these trip lines, the whole web vibrates. Deep within its burrow, the spider feels these vibrations with the help of the sensory hairs all over its body. It quickly lunges to the burrow's entrance. The spider grabs the unsuspecting prey with its pedipalps, drives its fangs into the creature's body, and injects a lethal dose of venom.

All that is left now is a short wait. The Sydney funnel-web's powerful venom goes to work on the prey's nervous system, causing a complete body malfunction that soon results in paralysis and death. After this occurs, the spider drags the unlucky victim down into its burrow. Like other spiders, it vomits digestive juices onto the corpse to dissolve the prey's flesh. The spider then sucks up its delicious liquid meal.

# Night Wanderers

Female Sydney funnel-web spiders stick to their burrows and hunt in this manner throughout most of their eight-year-plus lifetimes. For males, though, the pattern is different. Males also dig burrows and live there for their first four years or so, until they become mature adults. When this time arrives, the males leave their burrows and go searching for mates.

*Shoes are a favorite hiding place of Sydney funnel-web spiders. The spiders are also attracted to water, so they sometimes fall into backyard swimming pools.*

A male cannot always accomplish this goal in just one night. If the wandering spider has not found a female by the time morning comes, he hides away in a dark, cool spot and waits for the day to pass. At night, he emerges and resumes his search. He will do this over and over until he finally finds a mate.

This habit puts nearby humans in danger. Sydney funnel-webs on the move will take daytime shelter in any convenient, comfortable nook. This often includes areas around and even inside human homes. Woodpiles, rock gardens, trash heaps, sheds, porches, garages, shoes, and many other places make good hiding spots for a Sydney funnel-web spider. Anyone who

# ANTIVENOM

The antivenom for the Sydney funnel-web is made by injecting the spider's venom in tiny quantities into rabbits. Rabbits are immune to this spider's venom, so they feel no ill effects from the injection. But their bodies do develop antibodies, which are proteins that have the ability to fight the venom. The antibodies are separated from the rabbits' blood and made into medicines that help spider bite victims to survive.

Removing spider venom is called milking. This process involves sucking the venom out of a spider's fangs using a tiny pipette. Up to one hundred spiders must be milked to create one vial of antivenom, and bite victims generally receive two to four vials. It takes a lot of work to maintain an adequate supply of antivenom for public health needs.

But the Australian Reptile Park is up to the challenge. Scientists at this facility milk five hundred to seven hundred Sydney funnel-web spiders each week. The valuable liquid they extract is sent to a production facility where antivenom is made. This medicine works against the venom of many funnel-web spiders, not just the Sydney species. It is therefore an invaluable tool in Australia's medical arsenal.

sticks a hand into one of these places runs the risk of being bitten.

Swimming pools pose a particular danger. Sydney funnel-webs are attracted to water, so they often approach pools. Sometimes they fall in and are discovered by homeowners in the morning. The spiders appear dead—but they are actually very much alive. This arachnid's hairy body traps tiny air bubbles that the spider uses to survive up to thirty hours underwater. A person who carelessly removes one of these lifeless-looking creatures from a pool is in for a very nasty surprise.

## A Bad Bite

A Sydney funnel-web that is startled or cornered in this way will bite immediately. If the spider has time to react to an approaching person, though, it will put on a clear warning display. The spider rears up on its back legs and extends its long front legs toward the threat. At the same time, it pokes its fangs forward. Venom gathers in a large drop at each fang tip as the spider prepares to bite.

If a person comes closer despite this display, the spider has no choice but to attack. It moves forward and jabs its fangs into the person's flesh. The bite is so strong that it can puncture shoe leather or a human fingernail. Once the fangs are embedded, the spider injects its venom—and it does not hold back. Unlike many spiders, the Sydney funnel-web pumps as much poison as possible into its victim's body. It sometimes clings and bites over and over as it does this, leaving tiny puncture wounds up and down the skin, until it is pried loose.

At this point, the spider's venom goes to work. The Sydney funnel-web has neurotoxic venom that makes the victim's body lose control of its nerve impulses. The first symptoms of a severe bite appear within ten to thirty minutes and include tears, drooling, vomiting, and diarrhea. Soon afterward, the blood pressure rises sharply and then tumbles. The muscles spasm and the circulatory system falters. The victim slides into a coma and then, quickly, into death. From start to finish, the entire process can take as little as fifteen minutes.

*The needle-sharp fangs of the Sydney funnel-web spider (pictured) point downward and can be nearly .5 inches long. These spiders pump as much of their venom as possible into victims, sometimes biting them multiple times.*

The outlook for the bite victim depends partly on the amount of venom injected and partly on the bite location. Bites near the vital organs are usually worse than those on limbs. As one Australian expert puts it, "With a funnel web bite to the torso, you're dead. No other spider can claim that reputation."[4]

## The Human Toll

Luckily, despite the fact that the Sydney funnel-web spider is common near human populations, not many people have had encounters of this type. The spider's nocturnal and underground habits usually keep it away from people. In fact, a woman who did have the misfortune to be bitten by this creature in 2015 remembers the surprised reactions from hospital staff when she called for help. "The ambulance officers said I was only the second person [they had personally seen] in 16 years to get a funnel-web bite,"[5] she says.

Following her bite, this woman suffered twelve hours of agonizing pain but eventually made a full recovery. This is the case with most Sydney funnel-web envenomations (venom injections). Although there are an estimated thirty to forty human cases per year, only thirteen deaths have been recorded since 1927, when record keeping first started. There have been no human deaths since 1981, when an effective funnel-web antivenom (a substance that works as an antidote to spider venom) was introduced.

Just because there have been no recent deaths, though, does not mean people can relax their guard. Those who live near the Sydney funnel-web spider should be aware of this dangerous arachnid and take steps to keep themselves safe. With venom this toxic, any encounter could be a person's last.

# Chapter 5

# Eastern Mouse Spider

Members of the *Missulena* genus are commonly known as mouse spiders. Found mostly in Australia, these arachnids look much like the deadly Sydney funnel-web spider and have similar habits. They are not as dangerous as their lethal cousins, but they are venomous—and scientists believe that in the right circumstances, their bite could kill.

Scientists have identified somewhere between nine and seventeen species of mouse spider (official sources disagree on the number). Of these species, only one—the eastern mouse spider—has ever caused a reaction strong enough to kill a person. Although this spider's bite was not ultimately fatal to the stricken person, it easily could have been under different circumstances. Because of that fact, health officials consider this creature a life-threatening menace.

## Body Basics

The eastern mouse spider is often mistaken for the much-feared Sydney funnel-web spider because their body shapes and sizes are similar, and they are both dark in color. Like the funnel-web spider, the eastern mouse spider has a sturdy build, with a large, round abdomen, thick legs, and large chelicerae. The cephalothorax is shiny and black. The abdomen is furry and mostly dark brown.

A careful look, however, reveals subtle differences between the two species. The mouse spider is usually larger and stockier than the Sydney funnel-web spider, and its waist (the area where the cephalothorax and the abdomen meet) is wide instead of pinched inward. The mouse spider's legs and pedipalps are thicker and shorter, and the two spinnerets—which are long and prominent in the Sydney funnel-web—are much shorter as well. In terms of coloration, the mouse spider has a paler patch of fur in the middle of its back that the Sydney funnel-web lacks.

A close-up view shows even more distinguishing features. The mouse spider's head shape is different from that of the Sydney funnel-web spider, and its eight eyes are arranged differently. The fangs too are different: they crisscross each other whereas all funnel-web spiders have parallel fangs. Nonetheless, the fangs of both spiders are long, curved, and needle sharp.

## Home and Habits

An overlapping home range is another reason why the eastern mouse spider and the Sydney funnel-web are often confused. Both arachnids are native to Australia's eastern coast and are found in roughly the same areas.

To make matters even more confusing, both species are burrowers. Like their more dangerous cousins, mouse spiders tend to settle in areas with cool, damp, firm soil. They stay away from sandy beaches or places where hard-packed earth makes digging difficult. But otherwise, as long as the soil conditions are good, these spiders are not picky about their general area. They are equally happy deep in the woods or in a person's suburban garden. They are seldom found in cities, where suitable digging spots are hard to find.

One distinguishing feature of a mouse spider's burrow is the depth. These arachnids dig long, hard-packed holes ranging from about 8 to 20 inches (20 to 51 cm) from opening to end. People once thought that mouse spider lairs were even deeper — so deep, in fact, that they resembled mouse burrows. This belief gave the mouse spider its common nickname. Although scientists now know that the mouse spider's tunnels are

*Like the Sydney funnel-web spider, with which it is often confused, the eastern mouse spider (pictured) has a sturdy build and a large, round abdomen. However, the mouse spider is usually larger and stockier than the Sydney funnel-web.*

# THE EASTERN MOUSE
# SPIDER AT A GLANCE

- **Scientific name:** *Missulena bradleyi*
- **Scientific family: Actinopodidae**
- **Range: Eastern Australia**
- **Habitat: Soft-soiled ground in temperate areas**
- **Size (including legs): Up to 1.25 inches (3.2 cm)**
- **Diet: Crawling insects, arthropods, snails, small vertebrates**
- **Life span: Up to four years**
- **Key features: Stout body, wide waist, dark colors**
- **Deadly because: Potent venom**

not as impressive as once believed, the nickname has remained.

Whatever the length, all eastern mouse spider burrows have a similar shape and construction. The main shaft is straight and just wide enough for the spider to navigate comfortably. A small chamber is dug out to the side, with the entrance about midway along the shaft. The spider usually makes a plug out of silk or soil to use as a chamber door. The sealed chamber makes a safe, comfortable resting spot for the spider and, eventually, its eggs and spiderlings, if the burrow owner is a female.

The top of the burrow is also covered by one or sometimes two plugs that function like trapdoors. The plugs are camouflaged to look just like the surrounding ground and are very hard to spot. A few silk strands spread out around the doors, working as trip lines to alert the spider when other creatures draw near.

## On the Hunt

During the daytime, the eastern mouse spider rests inside its side chamber. Sealed off from the outer world by at least two doors, the spider stays safe, cool, and damp while the sun shines outside.

When nighttime arrives, the spider emerges from its chamber. It rests in its burrow with its head facing the closed trapdoors. The spider makes sure that the sensory hairs on its legs and body touch the trip lines that extend onto the ground outside the burrow. Motionless, the spider patiently waits for the vibration of the silken alert lines. The intruder might be any kind of crawling creature: an ant, a beetle, another spider, or even a small lizard or frog. It does not really matter. The eastern mouse spider is not a picky eater, and it will consume anything it can catch.

When the trip lines vibrate, the spider springs into action. It throws open the trapdoor that covers its burrow and leaps into the open air. It reaches out and seizes the unlucky creature that has wandered too close. It then uses its powerful jaws to drive its fangs into the prey's body. The spider injects a neurotoxic venom that damages the prey's nervous system. The creature quickly dies. The eastern mouse spider then drags the corpse through the trapdoor and down into the side chamber, where it will be liquefied and eaten at the spider's leisure.

On rare occasions, when prey is scarce, the eastern mouse spider may use a different hunting technique. Rather than waiting in ambush, it leaves its burrow and hunts actively for tasty morsels. The spider does this

*An eastern mouse spider raises its front legs in a warning posture. It was once thought that these spiders dig burrows comparable to those of mice, which led to their name. Although this belief has been proven false, the name has endured.*

only at night. It most commonly roams after periods of heavy rain, which can flood the spider's burrow and destroy its silken trip lines.

## Daytime Danger

Male mouse spiders also roam when they are looking for mates. But unlike the Sydney funnel-web spider, which travels only at night, male mouse spiders often emerge during the daytime. They are most often seen during the late summer to early winter months, especially after rain. They skitter about with their pedipalps stretched forward, using sensory organs on these appendages to scan the area for the telltale scents of nearby females.

If the male finds a mate, he will disappear into her burrow. Until this happens, though, the male will keep wandering—and this is a period of great danger for

# DRY BITES

The fact that the eastern mouse spider has highly toxic venom yet seldom sickens its human victims was once confusing to scientists. In one case, a mouse spider dug its fangs into a seven-year-old boy's finger and held on until it was crushed to death—yet the boy experienced no symptoms at all from the bite. In another case, a man received multiple bites from a swarm of mouse spiders that he disturbed in his basement. A few days later the man developed an infected area on one arm, but the wound was quickly cured with an antibiotic powder. He had no effects at all anywhere else in his body.

After some study, scientists have reached a verdict on this puzzling situation. They believe that mouse spiders prefer not to use their venom in defense. The vast majority of their bites are considered dry bites, which means the spider inserts its fangs but does not inject any venom. This is a lucky break for humans, who are vulnerable to this spider's deadly toxins.

nearby humans. The mouse spider is not aggressive, but like any creature, it will defend itself if it feels threatened. A person who accidentally comes too close is likely to get a nasty bite.

Before delivering this bite, the mouse spider puts on a display very similar to the one used by the Sydney funnel-web spider. It rears up on its back legs, extends its forelegs, and lifts its chelicerae to display its sharp fangs. This stance sends a clear warning: stay away.

If a person ignores this display, the spider will bite. Scientists do not know a great deal about the mouse spider's venom, but they do know that it contains a neurotoxin very similar to that of the Sydney funnel-web. In theory, the effects could be just as bad. As Australian Reptile Park manager Tim Faulkner says, "There's not a lot known . . . but it's a scary bite that you need to treat as if it's deadly."[6]

## Spider Statistics

So far, thankfully, this has not been the case. Twenty known cases of eastern mouse spider bites have not resulted in any human deaths. In most of these cases, the victims experienced no symptoms at all or only mild ones, including minor pain and swelling at the bite site. Several victims reported numbness near the bitten area that went away after a short time.

A few bite victims experienced more significant effects. Reported symptoms included sweating, infection of the bite site, and a pins-and-needles sensation in the nerves. Just one bite victim, a nineteen-month-old child, developed severe illness that included high blood pressure; muscle spasms; a rigid, painfully arched back; and unconsciousness. No mouse spider antivenom exists, so the toddler could not receive targeted treatment. But since funnel-web envenomation causes similar symptoms, the young patient received funnel-web antivenom in an emergency medical gamble. The medicine worked, and the toddler eventually made a full recovery.

This fact is good news for anyone who happens to encounter an eastern mouse spider lurking in a backyard garden. It means that in the worst-case scenario of a severe bite, medical treatment is available. And since the bite of the eastern mouse spider does not usually

*An Australian tree frog rests on a leaf. Unfortunately for frogs and other creatures, the eastern mouse spider is an ingenious trapper and hunter that is not picky about what it eats.*

cause such an extreme reaction, it is unlikely that the treatment would be needed in the first place.

But experts emphasize that the mouse spider should inspire caution nonetheless. One reason is the potential to misidentify this arachnid. A scientist might be able to tell the difference between a mouse spider and a lethal funnel-web with a single glance. For others, though, the task is considerably more challenging. As Tim Faulkner points out, "Most people would have no way of identifying between a mouse spider and a funnel-web."[7]

Another reason for caution is that studies show these spiders are potentially more toxic than funnel-web spiders. They have not killed anyone yet—but the strength of their venom seems perfectly capable of doing so.

The practical conclusion is that any big, black spider in eastern Australia—including the eastern mouse spider—should be treated with the utmost care. This arachnid may not be the deadliest predator in the spider kingdom, but it is a good one to avoid nonetheless.

# Chapter 6

# Indian Ornamental Tarantula

Judging solely by looks, tarantulas might be Earth's most terrifying spiders. These arachnids are hairy, stocky, fast, and horrifyingly large; in some species, the leg span is the size of a dinner plate. It is no wonder these creatures make spider-fearing people everywhere shudder.

Despite their fearsome size, though, most of the world's nine hundred tarantula species are harmless to people. This is especially true of the so-called New World tarantulas—species that are native to North, South, and Central America. The bite of these spiders is often compared to a bee sting in terms of both pain and effect.

The story is different when it comes to the Old World tarantulas. Native to Africa, Asia, Australia, and Europe, these spiders are much more venomous than their New World cousins—and among this group, the Indian ornamental tarantula stands out as the worst of the worst. A member of the highly venomous *Poecilotheria* genus, this spider is big, fast, and aggressive. It has not caused any known human deaths, but its bite has been known to cause severe illness requiring hospitalization. Scientists believe that under certain circumstances the Indian ornamental tarantula could, indeed, be a killer.

# Body Basics

Like many tarantulas, the Indian ornamental is big. Including the legs, it measures about 7 inches (18 cm) across—about the size of an adult human's spread-out hand. Males tend to be a bit smaller than females.

The Indian ornamental is not merely big. It is thickly built as well. This spider's central body, including both the cephalothorax and the abdomen, can measure over 3 inches (7.6 cm) long. The cephalothorax and abdomen are similar in size and shape and join at a slightly narrower waist. Eight hairy, pencil-thick legs protrude from the sides of the cephalothorax. At the front of the body are two long pedipalps, about half the length of the legs. Between the pedipalps are two thick, powerful chelicerae that end in dark, curved fangs nearly .5 inches (1.3 cm) long. The eight eyes are small and grouped together at the front of the head.

The Indian ornamental tarantula has striking coloration to go along with its big body. The spider's upper side is patterned in earthy shades ranging from black to brown, tan, and cream. The central body's background color is light brown, with markings of black and cream running the length of the body. The upper sides of the legs bear alternating stripes of black and cream.

A view from below reveals an entirely different color pattern. From this angle, the central body is a deep black broken by a wide reddish band across the abdomen. The legs bear brilliant black and yellow stripes along most of their length, and the final two joints on each leg are blue.

All parts of this spider, regardless of color, look hairy. The legs, pedipalps, chelicerae, and central body are

*The Indian ornamental tarantula poses a much bigger threat to humans than tarantulas native to the Americas. Its bite can cause illness severe enough to require hospitalization.*

covered with a thick layer of fine sensory bristles that look like the pelt of a small rodent. The feet are especially hairy. In fact, a close-up look shows that the Indian ornamental's feet actually have smaller hairs growing out of the larger ones. These extra hairs are an adaptation that gives this arachnid a good climbing grip.

## Home and Habits

A good grip is important for the Indian ornamental. This spider is arboreal, which means it lives in trees. It is abundant in the mountainous forests and plantations of southern and western India, where conditions are dry and temperatures are moderate.

Within these regions, Indian ornamentals commonly make their homes in the higher parts of trees rather than close to the ground. They prefer to settle in hollows and cracks. They will also move into abandoned bird or animal holes. In areas where good spots are plentiful, Indian ornamentals usually live alone. Where nesting areas are scarce, these spiders have been known to share living quarters and have sometimes been found in large groups.

Like all spiders, the Indian ornamental has spinnerets that it can use to make silk. The spider uses this silk to weave an irregularly shaped funnel that lines the walls and entrance of its lair. This web is not designed to be a hunting tool; it is made for the comfort and protection of the owner. The Indian ornamental rests in this web during the daytime hours. By avoiding the sun, it keeps its big body cool, well hydrated, and hidden from possible predators.

## On the Hunt

When evening arrives, the Indian ornamental becomes more active. The spider is ready to begin its nightly hunt for food.

# THE INDIAN ORNAMENTAL TARANTULA AT A GLANCE

- **Scientific name:** *Poecilotheria regalis*
- **Scientific family:** Theraphosidae
- **Range:** Southern and eastern India
- **Habitat:** Trees in wooded areas
- **Size (including legs):** 7 inches (18 cm)
- **Diet:** Mostly flying insects
- **Life span:** Up to fifteen years
- **Key features:** Large size, vivid markings
- **Deadly because:** Neurotoxic venom

The hunting method varies depending on the spider's hunger. A very hungry spider will leave its lair and wander off into the night in active search of food. A spider that has eaten recently, on the other hand, may just move to the front of its lair, where it can collect more information about its environment and possible nearby prey. It will use its sensory hairs to detect the sounds, smells, and vibrations made by approaching creatures. It also uses its eyesight to assess the environment. Although most tarantulas have poor eyesight, the Indian ornamental and other tree-dwelling species seem to have keener vision—enough, at least, to help them spot movement.

This movement might come from many different types of tree-dwelling creatures, and like most spiders, the Indian ornamental is not particular. It will attack anything that comes too close. Crawling insects, such as ants, beetles, and larvae, make a small but satisfying meal. Larger creatures, including other spiders, bats, and birds may also be taken. Mice and other small rodents sometimes become prey for the Indian ornamental as well, although these meals are much less common.

Prey of all types, whatever their size or speed, are taken in a similar way. The Indian ornamental gets close to the creature either by ambush (sitting and waiting) or by creeping up on the animal. When the spider is close enough, it uses its strong legs to propel itself forward in a mighty leap. Sometimes the spider catches the prey immediately. At other times, the prey escapes the Indian ornamental's leap and flees. In these cases, the spider runs after its intended meal with frightening speed.

*Small birds like the sunbird (pictured) provide ready prey for the Indian ornamental tarantula. The spider will eat anything ranging from ants and larvae to, occasionally, mice and other small rodents.*

# POPULAR PETS

Despite their dangerous venom, tarantulas of the *Poecilotheria* genus are popular pets among spider enthusiasts. Called pokies in the pet trade, these arachnids are dangerous but undeniably beautiful. The Indian ornamental tarantula is the most popular of the pokies due to its easy availability and calmer nature than others.

But even the calmest spider will bite, as many pet owners have discovered. Captive tarantulas must be cared for, which means their owners must feed them, clean their cages, and provide other services. Human hands are constantly being thrust into the spider's environment, and a nasty nip—or *tag* in spider owner terms—is sometimes the result.

A great deal of scientists' knowledge about the effects of the Indian ornamental's bite comes from these encounters since owners often report their symptoms on Internet message boards. Of course, the owners must survive in order to make these reports. So far no known tragedies have befallen any human keeper of this lovely yet potentially lethal spider.

More often than not, this high-stakes chase succeeds. The Indian ornamental is fast, agile, and able to outrun most prey. It grabs the creature and then uses its fangs to inject a killing dose of venom. The prey soon dies. It is dragged back to the spider's lair to be predigested in typical spider manner and then eaten.

## Ready to Attack

Like most animals, the Indian ornamental is not only a predator. It may become prey too. To protect itself from danger, this spider has an intimidating defensive display that it uses when a person comes too close.

A frightened Indian ornamental first turns to face the perceived threat. It rises up on its four back legs and raises its four front legs in the air. The raised legs clearly show the vivid yellow, black, and blue undermarkings. In nature, brightly colored creatures tend to be dangerous, so the coloration alone may convince predators to back off.

If it does not, the Indian ornamental has more tools at its disposal. The spider may bounce up and down, stamping its front feet on the ground. It may also rub spines together on its mouthparts and pedipalps to create a hissing sound.

If all of these efforts fail, the Indian ornamental will bite. The spider lunges forward in a lightning-quick leap and sinks its fangs into the offender's flesh. It may deliver a dry bite or a venom-laden one; there is no way to predict which one will occur. Then the spider withdraws its fangs and scuttles away while the victim waits to find out just how badly he or she has been bitten.

## Deadly or Not?

There has never been a reported human death from the bite of any tarantula, including the Indian ornamental. The effects of a full venom dose, however, can be extremely unpleasant and long lasting.

A recent study of twenty-six reported bites found ample evidence of this fact. The study describes one patient who developed severe muscle cramps, chest pain, and cardiac symptoms a few hours after a bite. The man went to the hospital, where he received muscle relaxers. Thanks to this treatment, the acute phase passed within a day, but the patient continued to suffer from flu-like symptoms that included joint pain and general malaise for three more weeks. Another man who was bitten by a different *Poecilotheria* species with venom very similar to that of the Indian ornamental suffered from nerve and joint pain that lasted for weeks, along with painful cramping of the calves that gave the man a pronounced limp.

These incidents show that the bite of the Indian ornamental should be taken seriously. The author of one

*An Indian ornamental tarantula raises its four front legs in a defensive display intended to repel a perceived threat. The spider's vivid coloring aids in warding off potential predators.*

study concluded that "*Poecilotheria* bites . . . are of medical importance to humans, even if hardly reported" and that, further, "the risk of *Poecilotheria* bites is strongly underestimated."[8]

Another study involving three bite victims, all otherwise healthy young men, found that severe effects from the bite of the Indian ornamental were more the rule than the exception. The doctors who treated the men stated, "Our patients' spasms were extremely distressing, incapacitating, and persistent. . . . In a child tarantula enthusiast, or even a debilitated elderly person, the severity of the symptoms we observed in these two healthy young men might well prove life threatening."[9]

Statements like these underscore the importance of caution when it comes to the Indian ornamental or any of its close relatives. Tarantulas may not usually be considered deadly—but in this particular case, it seems it would be wise to make an exception.

# Source Notes

## Chapter 1: Black Widow

1. Jackson Landers, "Dancing with Black Widow Spiders," *New York Times*, September 16, 2013. www.nytimes.com.

## Chapter 2: Brazilian Wandering Spider

2. Quoted in BBC News, "Pub Chef Bitten by Deadly Spider," BBC News, April 27, 2005. http://newsvote.bbc.co.uk.

## Chapter 3: Chilean Recluse

3. Quoted in Kate Nelson, "Warning: Graphic Pictures of Man's Flesh-Eating Spider Bite," London24, September 27, 2015. www.london24.com.

## Chapter 4: Sydney Funnel-Web Spider

4. Quoted in Joshua Robertson, "You Call That a Deadly Spider? Australia's Funnel Web Can Kill in 15 Minutes," *Guardian*, October 19, 2014. www.theguardian.com.

5. Quoted in Illawarra Mercury, "Halloween Horror for NSW Mum After Funnel Web Bite," *Sydney Morning Herald*, November 20, 2015. www.smh.com.au.

## Chapter 5: Eastern Mouse Spider

6. Quoted in Richard Noone, "Toddler Lucky to Survive Mouse Spider Bite While Holidaying with Par-

ents," *Daily Telegraph*, December 31, 2013. www
.dailytelegraph.com.au.

7. Quoted in Noone, "Toddler Lucky to Survive Mouse
Spider Bite While Holidaying with Parents."

## Chapter 6: Indian Ornamental Tarantula

8. Joan Fuchs et al., "A Verified Spider Bite and a Review of the Literature Confirm Indian Ornamental Tree
Spiders (Poecilotheria Species) as Underestimated
Theraphosids of Medical Importance," *Toxicon,* vol.
77, 2014, p. 74.

9. N. Ahmed et al., "Symptom in Search of a Toxin:
Muscle Spasms Following Bites by Old World Tarantula Spiders (Lampropelma nigerrimum, Pterinochilus
murinus, Poecilotheria regalis) with Review," *QJM: An
International Journal of Medicine*, vol. 102, no. 12,
pp. 851–57. http://qjmed.oxfordjournals.org.

**ambush:** A type of hunting in which the hunter hides and waits for prey to approach rather than actively pursuing prey.

**antivenom:** A medicine that counteracts the effects of spider venom. Also called antivenin.

**arachnid:** An arthropod of the class Arachnida, which includes spiders, scorpions, mites, and ticks.

**arachnophobia:** An extreme, irrational fear of spiders.

**camouflage:** Colors or patterns that help an animal to blend into its surroundings.

**chelicerae:** Strong jaw parts that bear the spider's fangs.

**habitat:** The natural home or environment of an animal.

**latrodectism:** The illness caused by the bite of *Latrodectus* spiders, including the black widow.

**loxoscelism:** The illness caused by the bite of *Loxosceles* spiders, including the Chilean recluse.

**neurotoxin:** A toxin that affects the nervous system.

**nocturnal:** Active mostly during the nighttime.

**pedipalps:** Appendages on the cephalothorax used for grasping, eating, sensing, and other activities.

**spinnerets:** A spider's silk-producing organs.

**toxin:** A poisonous substance produced by a living thing.

**venom:** A poisonous liquid made by many creatures, including spiders, that is injected by biting or stinging.

## Books

Richard A. Bradley, *Common Spiders of North America*. Berkeley: University of California, 2013.

Stephen Dalton, *Spiders: The Ultimate Predators*. Richmond Hill, Ontario: Firefly, 2011.

Bridget Heos, *Stronger than Steel: Spider Silk DNA and the Quest for Better Bulletproof Vests, Sutures, and Parachute Rope*. Boston: Houghton Mifflin Harcourt, 2013.

Marie Elisabeth Herberstein, ed., *Spider Behaviour: Flexibility and Versatility*. Cambridge, MA: Cambridge University, 2011.

Paul Hillyard, *The Private Life of Spiders*. Princeton, NJ: Princeton University, 2011.

Sara Latta, *Scared Stiff: Everything You Need to Know About 50 Famous Phobias*. San Francisco: Zest, 2014.

Sandra Markle, *Tarantulas: Supersized Predators*. Minneapolis: Lerner, 2012.

Richard S. Vetter, *The Brown Recluse Spider*. Ithaca, NY: Comstock, 2015.

# Websites

**Arachnopets** (www.arachnopets.com). This site is dedicated to the hobby of keeping spiders and other arachnids as pets. It includes a very interesting discussion board.

**British Tarantula Society** (www.thebts.co.uk). The world's oldest tarantula society, this organization provides information on tarantula keeping, research, conservation, and more.

**Planet Deadly** (www.planetdeadly.com). If something is dangerous or deadly in any way, it is probably profiled on this site.

**Spiders.us** (www.spiders.us). The home of an international spider community, this site offers general spider information with a North American focus.

**Spiderz Rule!** (www.spiderzrule.com). This site includes a wealth of information on many spider species and subjects.

# Picture Credits

# About The Author

Kris Hirschmann has written more than three hundred books for children. She owns and runs a business that provides a variety of writing and editorial services. She lives near Orlando, Florida, with her husband, Michael, and her daughters, Nikki and Erika.

# Bridesmaids' Club

KINGFISHER
LONDON & NEW YORK

Copyright © 2009 by Cathy Hopkins
Published in the United States by Kingfisher,
175 Fifth Ave., New York, NY 10010
Kingfisher is an imprint of Macmillan Children's Books, London.
All rights reserved.

Distributed in the U.S. by Macmillan, 175 Fifth Ave., New York, NY 10010
Distributed in Canada by H.B. Fenn and Company Ltd., 34 Nixon Road, Bolton,
Ontario L7E 1W2

Library of Congress Cataloging-in-Publication data has been applied for.

ISBN: 978-0-7534-6382-6

Kingfisher books are available for special promotions and premiums. For details contact:
Special Markets Department, Macmillan, 175 Fifth Avenue, New York, NY 10010.

For more information, please visit www.kingfisherpublications.com

Typeset by Intype Libra Limited
Printed and bound in the UK by CPI Mackays, Chatham ME5 8TD
1 3 5 7 9 8 6 4 2

Zodiac
Girls

# Bridesmaids' Club

## Cathy
## Hopkins

# Chapter One

# The Bridesmaids' Club

"Hey, Chloe, when do you think you'll hear from Marcie?" asked Demi as she cut out some pages from the February issue of *Weddings*.

"Any day now," I replied as I looked at the magazine over her shoulder. "I can't wait."

It was our monthly get-together of the Bridesmaids' Club, and just the three of us were there. Me and my friends Demi and Maryam. We always made it to the meeting, first Saturday morning of every month, held at one of our houses. We saw each other for lots of other things outside the club because we're best friends but our Bridesmaids' Club was a nonnegotiable event. Like Christmas day or Easter, it was part of our calendar. We started it back when we were nine, when we went to a wedding show in a nearby village called Osbury just for fun. We had such a great time trying all the samples and living the bridesmaids' dream that we decided we wouldn't leave it there. We'd start a club and talk about dresses, accessories, honeymoon locations, and all the rest every month. We put together files to be used by friends who needed wedding advice. We made ourselves experts. Other girls came and went as their various relatives got married, but we three, we were regulars—rain or shine, wedding or no wedding.

My mom teases me that the club is an obsession, but then my whole family teases me about everything, probably because I'm the youngest and more romantic and into girl stuff than any of my three career-driven older sisters. Maybe I'm into it all because of my sign—not that I particularly believe in astrology and all that stuff, but I did read somewhere that Libras are known for their love of beauty. That's me. I do like nice things, always have, and everything to do with weddings is fairy-tale lovely.

"I wonder how he'll do it," said Maryam. "Is he the down-on-one-knee type?"

She was talking about my sister Marcie's boyfriend, Geoff. Marcie had been dating him for about six months. He'd swept her off her feet in a whirlwind romance after she'd split up with Sam, who had broken her heart. When Geoff booked a long weekend in Paris, we all suspected that this was it. Proposal time.

I shrugged in answer to Maryam's question. "I hope so. Marcie likes a bit of romance when the mood takes her."

Demi and Maryam nodded. Marcie was an honorary member of the Bridesmaids' Club and secretly loved all that romantic stuff. She was my favorite sister, the best in the world, and even though she didn't live at home anymore, she was around a lot and always made time for me. The only blip had been when she was dating Sam. I was so relieved when she broke things off with him and met Geoff. Sam used to tease me about the Bridesmaids' Club, which he thought was a joke.

My other two sisters, Jane and Clare, think I'm too immature to waste their days off on, so I was thankful that I had at least one sister who was occasionally up for shopping trips and could be persuaded into sessions of DIY pampering, painting nails, and trying out face masks. Marcie was great. She'd always been there to drive me and my friends to the movies, to play practical jokes on us, to see the latest chick flick, then laugh, gossip, and eat French fries on the way home. And I'd seen her watch romantic movies and blub even though she tried to hide it. Until, that is, what I call her lost period, when she was with Mr. Sam Lycra Shorts Hendy, the thunder from down under (he was from Australia). She totally changed when she was with him and it was bye-bye Marcie, hello Lara Croft, action girl. With Sam, she'd been white-water rafting, camping under the stars, climbing mountains. My Marcie, who didn't even own a pair of sneakers pre-Sam, who only stayed at five-star luxury hotels on vacation and thought sleeping in tents was for losers! I was so with her on that—not that I'd stayed in many five-star hotels, but I knew that when I was older I would rather sleep in the softest linen and have a bathroom with fluffy white towels than camp out in a damp sleeping bag in a tent and have to go to the bathroom in some stinky bucket. All part of being Libran apparently. We don't like to rough it. Anyway, Marcie's back to normal, thanks to Geoff.

She never admitted to Sam that she was a member of the Bridesmaids' Club because of his views about weddings. He thought that marriage and all that went with it was a waste of time. Marcie didn't tell Clare or Jane either, because she didn't want to be seen as an airhead who was easily carried away by a bit of sparkle. As if. She's got a degree in quantum physics. Our whole family is brainy, me included. I am always top of our class in most subjects. Mom and Clare are lawyers, and Jane lectures at the local university—her subject is statistics. Like, how dull is that? And Dad is a scientist (he doesn't live with us anymore—he and Mom are divorced, and he lives with his new wife in Florida).

Clare and Jane had practically ruined any chance for me to be a bridesmaid. "No time to waste on men," said Clare soon after she left home. "I don't need anyone to share my life with. I am perfectly

4

happy on my own. My career is what matters." She does date men occasionally, usually guys she meets online, but they never last. I think she eats them for breakfast or buries them under her patio—she sees men as disposable and not completely necessary. Jane does have a steady boyfriend, and after they had been together a few years, I thought maybe I'd get my chance to be a bridesmaid. But no, she announced that they don't need a piece of paper to show that they are serious, so they live together as "partners." I did everything I could to talk her into getting married, but she cut me off, saying that Western culture was steeped in materialism and that marriage was just another consumerist event to rob decent people of their money by feeding them an unrealistic fantasy. Like, *whoa*, okay, so that might be true, but I can also see the other side. The fun side. Needless to say, Sam got along well with Jane and Clare because they all shared the same views about marriage.

At one time, I had hoped that Mom might remarry, but she swears that she never will. She says that men let you down. I think my dad's leaving hurt her and my sisters more than they let on. He left when I was still a baby, so I don't miss him because I don't remember him. All I know is that, because of him, my mom and sisters are suspicious of men.

What it all means is that I've never once been in a

wedding. It's so not fair. Demi and Maryam have both been bridesmaids. Demi *twice*, once with her sister, Rose, and once with her aunt Mags. But soon, very soon, it might be my turn, and it'll be utterly FABulous. Demi's aunt was a winter bride, and her sister got married in the spring, and the wedding Maryam was in took place in the fall, so that would leave summer for me. I wouldn't want to copy what has already been done.

Not that I wasn't prepared in case Marcie and Geoff chose winter for the big day—the wedding could be held in a rich hotel in New York City or maybe Boston. I could just see it. It would be snowing. Marcie would arrive in a horse-drawn carriage. She would be wearing ankle-length white velvet with a long cloak, a crown of ivy on top of her flowing hair. Very medieval princess. If it was during the summer, we could jet off to some fabulous island: the Caribbean, or maybe Hawaii or even Mexico. Yeah. We'd be jet-set cool. I had maps and stacks of brochures showing couples kissing in the surf at sunset. Marcie could wear a shimmer of ivory silk cut on the bias, possibly backless to show off her perfect, even tan, with her hair swept up at the back in a sophisticated style and sprinkled throughout with tiny pearls and flowers. Or, if they didn't want to travel far, we could book some gorgeous inn in the country, very romantic, Marcie in an off-the-shoulder sheath dress. She'd look fab. I'd look fab. Whatever the season or location, I would follow her wearing something stunningly original. *Not* lilac. Or candy pink. Or anything with mutton sleeves. Or bows. The guests would gasp. A wall of cameras would click. We'd be featured in all the mags where page after page would gush about how we made the most *gorgeous* wedding party ever seen. And they'd be right, too. Marcie cleans up well when she can be bothered to make the effort, and I am five foot four, have long legs, and shoulder-length blond hair. Perfect bridesmaid material.

Not that Demi and Maryam aren't pretty. They are. Maryam is dark-skinned with gorgeous black curls to her shoulders and the most amazing huge brown eyes. She looked like a Caribbean princess in an ivory dress when her sister got married. Demi is pale and tall with long, dark straight hair. Her sister did the pink thing for her bridesmaids, and Demi made it work by getting a spray tan the day before so that she didn't look washed out at all (pale pink can be a hard color to wear unless you're a blond, like me).

A lot of our friends at school who were drop-in members of the Bridesmaids' Club had already had their big days, too. Susie Jenson had been a bridesmaid last spring—that wedding was held in an exclusive country club. She was passing around the photos for weeks afterward. I oohed and aahed as you do, but I was thinking, *Just wait until it's my turn. Then you'll see something really special.* And then it was Tara Peters's turn. A rhapsody in shocking pink. Talk about tack city! There are some shades of pink that just don't work for a wedding. Jess Lewis was next: cream with too many ribbons and bows, for a shepherdess kind of look. Bows? Double yuck.

I really do intend to make Marcie's wedding the best ever. *Ever.* And Geoff, unlike Sam, never once laughed or teased me when he found out about the Bridesmaids' Club. He was genuinely interested when he heard about it and asked how it got started and what we did and so on.

So I can't wait to hear what Marcie and Geoff want. Not that it will be a problem whatever they choose. There isn't anything about weddings that I don't know about. I've been collecting ideas for years, ready for my turn—and now it may be about to happen. My brides-maid album is bursting at the seams. I add to it all the time—I cut dresses out of *Brides* magazine or anything else that I see in ads or on the Internet. I have fabrics, dress designs, jewelry, shoes, hairstyles, veils, locations for the ceremony, and locations for the honeymoon—every aspect of weddings there is. Best of all, Marcie has always been open to all my suggestions, whether for table arrangements, flowers for the church, choice of appetizers, or the best songs for dancing. I have vintage cars, limos, open carriages, snow sleds . . . you name it, lined up. Marcie was happy to leave all the details to me. All that had been missing until now was the groom, and that I couldn't help her with.

For a short time, when she was single after breaking up with Sam, she was so heartbroken that she said she would never date again, and I was just beginning to wonder if she was doomed to be alone forever when along came Geoff. He was tall, dark, and handsome. A friend of hers introduced them at a dinner party, and there was no going back. I was so relieved. Sam had been wrong for Marcie, and not only because of his love for sports and adventure vacations, but also because he was commitment shy (which was the real reason they broke up) and, according to Marcie, terrible at communicating his feelings. Even though Marcie went along with the baseball, hiking, surfing, tennis, and climbing, I figure she wouldn't have been able to keep it up for a lifetime.

But Geoff fits the role of handsome prince perfectly, and Marcie says he's very happy to talk about feelings. Plus, he always lets her have her own way and make all the decisions about how they are going to spend their time. When the Paris trip was announced a few weeks ago, I just knew that my life's ambition was about to be achieved and that the fairy-tale wedding was set to rock and roll.

Demi clicked her fingers in front of me. "Hey, dreamer! Earth to planet Chloe," she said. "We're supposed to be thinking about that huge project that's due at the end of the year. You do want to graduate from eighth grade, don't you? Maryam and I would hate to go on to high school without you."

"Yeah, Chloe. We'd be lost without you. Have you chosen a topic yet?"

"Ugh! Don't remind me," I groaned. In order to be promoted to high school, all the eighth graders at my school have to write and perform a massive presentation about potential career paths. I hadn't even begun to work on it. Every time someone brought it up, I felt sick to my stomach.

Demi and Maryam were waiting for my answer. I put my hands up as if to say I didn't know. Indecision is one of my biggest problems. Always has been (another Libran trait, according to my *Girl in the City* magazine's astrology page). I never know what I want aside from being in the Bridesmaids' Club. "I can't decide. It's okay for you guys—Maryam, you've wanted to be a fashion designer since the moment you were born, and, Demi, you've got your photography."

Maryam nodded. "Yeah. Writing the proposal was a cinch. All I have left to do is interview a professional designer and somehow convince them to let me work at their company for a while."

"Chloe, you must have some ideas," said Demi. "You're going to run out of time."

"Nope. Don't know. Mom thinks I'd be a good lawyer because I'm good at seeing both sides of an argument but I think, lawyer? Boring. And course Dad wrote to me and advised me to follow in his footsteps and choose science, but no way do I want to be stuck in a laboratory all my life, and why should I listen to him? He never comes to visit, and he's not really part of my life, so why should he get a say? I wish everyone would get off my case. Like, I'm fourteen—I have years to decide."

"Well, if you want to pass—" said Demi.

"I know what I'll do!" I cut Demi off mid-sentence. "I'll say I want to be a street sweeper and study collecting garbage," I said. Neither of them laughed. "Oh, come on, guys, chill out. I have enough with Mom, Dad, and three sisters nagging me about what I should do and how hard I have to study to get there without you two doing it as well." But they were right. Mr. Mooney would never pass someone trying to fake a career choice. This whole conversation was making me very nervous.

At that moment, from the back pocket of my jeans, my phone beeped that I had a text. I pulled it out and glanced at the screen. Demi and Maryam looked at me expectantly.

I nodded. "Marcie."

# Chapter Two

# Wedding Show

"Okay," said Demi as we took in the hundreds of booths in the vast tent that had been decorated from corner to corner with pink sparkly banners and hundreds of heart-shaped balloons. "Let's start over here and go up one aisle, down the next, and so on, so that we don't miss anything."

Maryam and I gave her a salute. "Aye-aye, captain," I said. It was a week after Marcie had announced her engagement, and we were at the annual wedding show in the park in Osbury. Marcie had sounded very happy when I spoke to her. I wanted to know all the details, but she said that her phone card was running low, so although she could confirm that she was definitely engaged to be married and that they wanted to do it in June, she'd fill me in on the rest later. I was dying to know how he'd proposed. She promised she'd tell me everything when she came home next, and I could hardly wait.

In the meantime, there was the wedding show. It was held every year around Valentine's Day, and Demi and Maryam and I hadn't missed a show since we were nine. Already I could see some familiar faces. A pretty brunette at a jewelry stall waved, so we trooped over.

"Hi, Chantelle," we chorused.

"Hey, girls," she said. "You here again?"

"Wouldn't miss it," said Demi.

"And this year, *I* have a wedding to plan," I said. "A very special wedding."

"Who?" asked Chantelle.

"My sister Marcie," I replied. "Her boyfriend took her to Paris to propose."

Chantelle sighed. "*How* romantic. I'd *love* to be taken to Paris."

"I know. Me, too. I'm going to make her relive every detail when she gets back."

Chantelle laughed. "So what kind of wedding does she want?"

"Not sure yet. She's still away but she's coming over next weekend for Sunday lunch and we'll discuss it then."

"We're here to get ideas," said Demi.

"Get the ball rolling," said Maryam.

"The show's such perfect timing," I said.

"Your sister is a lucky girl," said Chantelle, "having you to do her research. You be sure and tell her about my jewelry, won't you? Though I suppose if he's already asked her to marry him then she's got the ring?"

I nodded. "I guess, though I haven't seen it yet."

"I'd better get back to work, girls," said Chantelle when a customer began poking at her display. "Enjoy the show, and check out Aisle H. There are some new people down there. They call themselves Celestial Weddings. I haven't seen any of them before, and they look like a fun bunch."

"Aisle H. Will do," I said.

We set off to roam through the booths, and soon we were caught up in the usual show frenzy as vendors thrust brochures and leaflets at us and various sales-people beckoned us to come and sample their goodies.

"You're so lucky to have a wedding this year," said Demi as she looked through an album at one booth showing floral arrangements for the ceremony.

"I know," I said and I gave myself a hug. "I've been waiting *all* my life for this." I loved the annual wedding show. I loved it even more than Christmas and birthdays, more than Easter with all the chocolate. I loved the glamour, how pretty everything was. I loved the dream. It was true, everything my sisters said about the wedding industry selling a fantasy, but that was exactly what I *liked*—that for one day someone could be transported into another world, an enchanted world where the bride was a princess and the groom was her prince. A world where everyone looked their most beautiful and happy, where people danced merrily, butterflies flitted, and doves cooed, where there was music and flowers and delicious food, a yummy scrummy cake, and a celebration of love. So my family dissed it. In my opinion, they were *seriously* missing out on one of life's true joys.

We cruised the booths for an hour or so, tried every freebie, greeted old friends: Jason promoting honeymoon destinations, Elena selling Belgian chocolates, Moira at Tux and Tails, Arthur advising on wedding invitations, Georgina on dresses for the mothers-in-law, Anna Lee on shoes. We chomped on samples of wedding cake, oohed and aahed over the dresses modeled in a fashion show, sat in a white wedding limo, and sipped on sparkling apple juice. We entered every prize drawing. It was part of the fun. There were prizes from the cheap to the spectacular— for makeup, makeovers, jewelry, cakes, cars, a weekend in the Caribbean for a lucky bride and groom—you name it. The fair organizers always announced the winners up on stage at the end of the show and made a big fuss over them. So far, none of us had won anything, but that didn't stop us from entering every year.

We tried on a variety of tiaras and turned our noses up at anything we thought looked cheap or tacky.

"*So* downmarket," said Demi with a disapproving sniff as we surveyed one stall that sparkled with eye-dazzling bling. I nodded in agreement with her but

I didn't even mind the tack. I felt so happy. This was my world. I loved every minute of it and could never understand why everyone else didn't feel the same way.

Next was a booth with men's aftershaves, and we had a sniff of a few. Some smelled too strong, like potpourri with a slice of lemon. Yuck! I prefer the subtler scents, the classics, like Chanel or Armani. Marcie once said that Sam smelled like the sea—sand dunes and salty air. She said it was one of the things she liked so much about him—his natural scent. Pff! That wouldn't have been right for a wedding. Eau de Sand Dune. I am sure that Geoff will wear Armani on the big day if we tell him to because he does everything Marcie asks.

"So, what do you think so far?" asked Demi when we reached Aisle H, where I could see that Chantelle had been right: there did appear to be some new faces.

"Hmm," I said. "I've seen a few things I think Marcie might like. I think that since she's getting married in June, we should go for the classic summer look. An ivory sheath of silk. Marcie's got the perfect slim figure for that kind of dress."

Demi sighed. "She's going to look so beautiful."

"I know," I agreed. *And so am I*, I thought. I'd seen a number of bridesmaids' dresses that would look great on me. It depended on what colors Marcie wanted and whether she wanted just me as her bridesmaid or if she wanted Demi and Maryam, too. It was going to be fun deciding everything. Usually having to make choices is my worst nightmare because I can never make up my mind, but when it comes to planning a wedding, the millions of choices to be made make it all the more enjoyable.

We began to walk down Aisle H, looking at the new booths. They each had the same logo on a banner behind their booth. It said "Celestial Weddings" and had stars and planets whizzing around the words. *That sounds good*, I thought as we took a closer look. One booth had samples of wedding invitations, all tasteful and elegant. I took a sample and, for future reference, made a note of the name of the designer: Hermie at Mercury Communications, part of Celestial Weddings. Another booth had a fabulous array of wedding food, displayed by a jolly-looking man who introduced himself as Joe Joeve and then offered us a sample of cake. I took a piece and bit into it. It was light and melted in my mouth with a burst of white chocolate.

"Wow!" I said. "This is divine."

He beamed back at me and gave me his card. "Europa Catering for Celestial Weddings," it said, "Food Fit for the Gods."

Demi stopped at a booth that appeared not to have a representative. "Be a goddess for a day," said a poster underneath the Celestial Weddings banner hanging at the back of the booth. On the table in front there was a large white book with silver edging. I flipped it open to see a portfolio of dresses.

"Fabulous," said Maryam as I looked at the first page. It was my favorite kind of wedding dress—a simple sheath cut on the bias, elegant and classic.

"And that model is stunning," said Demi.

I took a closer look. Demi was right. The model was amazing looking. "Wow! She's a good advertisement, isn't she? She actually *looks* like a goddess." We turned page after page of the most fabulous dresses, all modeled by the same woman. Each dress was beautifully cut and enhanced with extras of lace and mother-of-pearl sewn in here and there, just enough to make them different from others at the show, but not so much that they stood out as over the top.

"She's not a model I've ever seen before," said Maryam. "Maybe she's new to the business?"

I looked more closely at the book to find her name. "Designs by Nessa, modeled by Nessa" it said at the bottom of the page. How cool, one name—like she didn't need a surname.

"These are the best designs I have *ever* seen in all our years of coming to the show," I said as I looked around. "So graceful."

Demi and Maryam nodded in agreement. "And look," said Demi as she picked up a leaflet from the table. "She does makeovers, too. 'Hair and makeup by Nessa.'"

"I wonder who she is and if she's here at the show," I said.

Maryam suddenly tugged on my arm. "Hey, look at this," she said, pulling me toward the next stall.

"Horoscopes!" said Demi, and she began to read the board at the right-hand side of the table. "'Plan your perfect day by the stars.'"

"Wow, astrology! I've never seen a booth advertising that here before, have you?"

"I know. I'm the first. Ridiculous, isn't it?" said a male voice.

We turned to see a tall, slim man standing to our right. He was dressed in a white sparkly jumpsuit with his silver-white hair spiked up. He was beautiful in an elfin-prince kind of way, and he looked like he belonged in a sci-fi or fantasy movie. He certainly didn't look like any of the other vendors, all of whom were dressed in traditional wedding outfits or in ordinary clothes. This man looked like he'd landed from a distant planet.

"I'd say that it's very important to make sure you're getting married on a day when the stars are lined up favorably, wouldn't you?" he continued.

"Yes. Of course. Yes," I said. "I never thought of that." I didn't know a lot about astrology apart from a few things about Librans, but I did know that some days were supposed to be good and some not so good according to where the Sun or Moon was.

"I mean, can you imagine if you'd set the day and, say, Saturn and Mars were square to each other? Or even worse, Saturn and Venus in opposition—that might be a disaster. Venus is the planet of love and harmony, you know. It's very important that she's in the right place on someone's special day."

I felt slightly in awe of this odd man but had to agree he was talking sense. I had read once in Mom's newspaper that one of the presidents was said to have consulted an astrologer regularly, and if that worked for important things like running a country, then it was probably a good idea to consult an astrologer about planning a wedding.

"How can we get a horoscope done?" I asked.

"Here," said the man. "My name's Uri, and I can do it for you right now." He indicated a computer in the booth. "All I need from you is the date, place, and time of birth of the bride and groom."

"The bride's my sister. I know she was born on August ninth, not far from here, but I don't know what time, and I don't know the wedding date yet—she just got engaged and they haven't set the date yet, although I think it will be June. And, um, Geoff's birthday is . . . let me think, November thirtieth . . .

Oh no, that's Sam's, um, he was her ex. Geoff . . . Geoff's birthday? March. Yeah. March seventh, that's it, and he was born in Connecticut and lived there all his life with his mom until she died last year."

Demi sighed. "Lucky he met Marcie so soon after, poor thing," she said.

"Yeah. He might have been really lonely otherwise," I agreed.

Uri beamed. "Okay. So the bride is a Leo. They are compatible with other fire signs usually—Aries and Sagittarius. Did you say that the groom's birthday was November thirtieth? That's good. That would make him a Sagittarius. Leos and Sagittarians are a *great* match."

"No. No. November was Sam's birthday. Geoff is March seventh."

Uri frowned. "He's a Pisces then."

"Is that a good match?" asked Demi.

"Um . . . I need the exact time to do it properly," Uri mumbled.

"Why?" asked Demi.

"You can find out only what your Sun sign is from your date of birth. You see, your Sun sign changes every month, but your Moon sign changes every two days, and your rising sign changes every two hours. All the different factors are what make each chart completely unique."

"Whoa! Information overload. Sun sign? Moon

sign? Rising sign? I thought there were only twelve signs of the zodiac," said Demi.

"True," said Uri. "Aries, Taurus, Gemini, Cancer, Leo, Virgo, Libra, Scorpio, Sagittarius, Capricorn, Aquarius, and Pisces. But that's only the tip of the iceberg. They each have ten planets that affect them, not just the Sun—if that was all there was to it, everyone born under the sign of Capricorn would be exactly the same, wouldn't they? Astrology is more of a science, which is why I need accurate data: date of birth, time, and place. The place is important because someone born in California and another born in New York at the same time on the same day will also have different characteristics because the stars will all be at different angles in relation to those spots on Earth. Right?"

"I guess," said Demi. "I never thought of that."

"Can you do our horoscopes, too?" asked Maryam.

Uri nodded. "Sure," he said. He looked at me. "You're a Libran, right?"

I nodded.

"Do you know much about your sign?" he asked.

"A bit," I replied. "Like we're supposed to be romantic and like beautiful things."

Uri nodded. "Indeed. Librans are a nice sign. Charming is another trait."

I gave him what I hoped was my most winning

smile and he laughed.

"Charming, easygoing, sociable, lovers of beauty," he continued. "They love to dress up, like the good things in life, and have a great eye for quality and true style." I curtsied to the others. It felt good having such complimentary things said about me. "On the other hand, every sign has a dark side, and for Librans, it's that they can be indecisive and changeable."

"That's true," I said. "I can never make up my mind about *anything*."

"They can also be easily influenced, they don't like being rushed, they can be self-indulgent, shallow—"

"Hey," I said. "Shallow?"

"Shallow and self-indulgent," he said.

"That's not very kind," I said.

"And they don't like to be criticized either," said Uri. "Oh no. They can be bossy, too, because they like their own way."

Demi and Maryam giggled and nodded.

"Generally, they are a lovely sign though," said Uri. "Easygoing and good company."

"Huh!" I said. I wasn't sure what to make of it. I certainly wasn't feeling very easygoing after having been told that I was shallow and self-indulgent.

Luckily Uri shifted his focus and looked at Demi. "Gemini?" She nodded. He looked at Maryam. "Sagittarius." She nodded. While they chatted with

23

Uri, I got out my cell phone and tried Marcie's number. It went straight to voicemail.

"I'll call home," I said during a break in the conversation. "Mom'll think I'm nuts though. In fact, all of my family would laugh if they knew I was doing horoscopes."

Demi, Maryam, and I found a quiet spot in the tent, and each of us phoned home. As I had expected, Mom gave me the usual inquisition. "Why do you need your time of birth? You're not supposed to give personal details to a stranger because they could be used for identity theft."

"Oh, Mom, I know that. But even if someone did steal my identity, what are they going to steal from me? I haven't exactly got millions in the bank."

"Then tell me what it's for."

"I want to get my horoscope done—"

"Horoscope! That nonsense. Oh, for heaven's sake, Chloe."

"It's not nonsense. Actually, if you gave it a chance, you'd realize that it's, um . . . scientific. And I want to do Marcie's, too. Oh, come on, Mom, tell me my time of birth. Uri can't do my chart without it."

"Uri. Uri! Who's Uri?"

"He's the astrologer."

"Good grief, Chloe. Where are you?"

"The wedding show. I told you."

As Mom launched into a lecture against astrology, I could see that Demi and Maryam were writing down their details, having clearly gotten them from their parents. Demi went over to Uri, and I watched as he punched numbers into his computer. Seconds later, crisp sheets of paper printed out and he handed them to her. He then took Maryam's info, and she got her horoscope, too.

"Demi and Maryam's moms have given their details," I said as soon as Mom paused to draw breath.

"Then they are very foolish."

"Please, Mom. I'll do dishes for a year."

"Bargaining won't get you anywhere."

"Two years."

She was quiet for a few moments, and then I heard her laugh. "Deal," she said. "You were born at six P.M. in the hospital just outside Osbury." I knew she'd give in. She hated washing dishes. I had realized when I was about seven that I could use it as a bargaining tool.

"Thanks, Mom. You're the best. Oh, and can you give me Marcie's as well? I'll do the dishes forever."

"Forever. You do realize that I will hold you to that, don't you? Now, Marcie? Ooh, let me think. She took a long time to arrive, let me remember, yes, August ninth, about . . . about . . . five thirty A.M.-ish. I can't quite remember."

After the call, I clicked my phone shut and wrote

down the information on the back of one of the leaflets I had picked up. When I got back to Uri, he was busy with a very loud group of people who were demanding their charts and giggling and generally making a big scene.

He took Marcie's details, glanced at them, then shook his head. "Hmm. And her fiancé is Pisces?"

"Yes. Is there anything wrong with that?"

"I'll get back to you," he said as the man from the loud group called him.

I felt so disappointed as I walked away. There was less than half an hour to go before the show was finished, and the family that was crowding around Uri looked like they could be there for at least that long. Demi and Maryam were studying their charts and looking pleased with them. They wanted to go and sit down and get a drink while they read them thoroughly. I went with them and we bought mango smoothies and sat down to read. Demi is Gemini with Libra rising.

"Maybe that's why we get along," she said to me.

"And I am Sagittarius with Gemini rising," Maryam said. "Maybe that's why we get along, Demi."

Demi nodded. "The rest of it reads like gobbledegook, doesn't it?"

"Yeah," said Maryam, and she folded her pages

and put them in her bag. "Way complicated."

At the front of the tent, we could hear various prize winners being called up on to the stage. We pulled out our raffle tickets and got ready.

"There goes my silver limo," said Maryam, tossing one of her tickets into the trash can when the winner was announced to be number 202, Margaret Beesley.

"There goes my trip to St. Lucia," said Demi, and she tossed a ticket aside as another winner was announced.

A few more names were called, and soon all our raffle tickets were in the trash can.

Demi and Maryam sighed. "Ah well, there's always next year," I said.

"And now . . ." There was a burst of trumpets. "Will Chloe Bradbury come to the stage, please," said a female voice over the loudspeakers.

"Ohmigod!" we chorused in unison.

I felt a rush of adrenalin. "Maybe I won something!" I looked in my purse to check for a stray ticket, but they were all gone. "Oh no, I might have lost the ticket! I don't have any left."

"Chloe Bradbury, please come to the stage," said the announcer again.

I was about to dive into the trash can to retrieve the tickets we'd chucked away, but Maryam and Demi herded me toward the stage.

"Come on! Someone just called your name again. Let's go see what you've won before they give your prize to someone else," said Demi.

Uri was standing mid-stage waiting for me. "Come on," he beckoned to me.

I grabbed Demi and Maryam's hands and pulled them up the stage steps with me, but they pushed me forward to take my prize on my own.

"What did I win?" I whispered to Uri when I reached him.

He tapped the side of his nose and winked. As he did, the lights in the tent went down, bathing everyone in a soft pink glow. Soft spacey music began to play, a harp and tinkling bells. And then laser lights blasted on, swirling around the stage and the tent, and the space music grew more upbeat. Uri announced to the audience, "Chloe Bradbury, YOU are this month's Zodiac Girl!"

From somewhere up high, white balloons were released. At that moment, the blond woman who was the model in the goddess book stepped out from the left onto the stage. I recognized her immediately. Nessa. I gasped. She really *did* look like a goddess and was even more beautiful in the flesh than in her photos. She was tall, with milky, white skin, the most perfect heart-shaped face and sky-blue eyes. She was dressed in one of her wedding dresses, a white off-the-shoulder sheath with one strap of tiny crystals. The audience cheered, and she waved back, every inch a celebrity. She came over and placed a tiara on my head then put a white sash over my shoulders with the words "Zodiac Girl" written in silver sequins.

"Congratulations," she said in a distinct Southern accent, and she handed me two blue boxes tied with silver ribbon.

I felt as if I was in a dream. On cloud nine. I could hardly breathe for excitement. In front of the stage, a sea of happy faces beamed back at me.

"Zodiac Girl? What does that mean?" I asked.

"Open your presents, darlin'," she said. "You'll see."

I untied the ribbon on the first box. Inside was a silver chain that had a tiny charm with the symbol of the scales, which I knew from my *Girl in the City* magazine represented Libra. Nessa took it from the box and put it around my neck while people cheered again. I opened the second box. Inside was the smallest cell phone I had ever seen. It was turquoise with a beautiful opal stone above the dialing pad. To my right, Demi and Maryam gave me the thumbs-up.

"Thank you," I said to Nessa.

"You're welcome," she replied. "It's no ordinary phone. It's a *zodiac* phone." She gently ushered me to the wings of the stage, and activity resumed in the tent as some general announcements were made over the loudspeaker.

Nessa indicated the phone. "You're a very, very lucky girl. To be chosen as a Zodiac Girl is a rare honor. For one month the stars will come to your aid, and I, Nessa, the embodiment of Venus, will be your guardian. I'll be there for you whenever you need me. You can reach me or one of the other planets from your zodiac phone. We want your special month to be magical and memorable."

"Thank you," I whispered, although I had no idea what she had said. I was too busy gazing at her. I was completely star-struck. I had never met a celebrity before, and my mind seemed to have gone blank.

The rest of the show felt like a blur. Nessa disappeared with Uri, people started packing up their booths, and all too soon it was time to go home. Demi and Maryam were impressed with my phone and necklace, and both said how jealous they were that they hadn't been picked as Zodiac Girls.

"I'm going back to find that man," said Maryam, and she set off for Aisle H. Demi and I followed, and we caught up to Uri just as he was about to leave on a unicycle.

"Hey, can we be Zodiac Girls, too?" Maryam asked.

He shook his head. "No, I'm sorry. One month, one

girl," he said. Then he looked over at me and handed me a piece of paper. "Here's your horoscope, Chloe. Every month somewhere on the planet, according to the alignment of the stars, one girl, and one girl only, is chosen to be a Zodiac Girl. Too bad Mercury will be retrograde for your first week. Mercury is the planet of communication. Hmm. With the line-up of stars in your chart, Chloe, it could be tricky for the first seven days. Make sure you don't lose your phone. That's the sort of thing that happens when Mercury is going backward. We'll be in touch if we can. In the meantime, expect the unexpected. Toodles!"

And with that, he rode off on his unicycle.

# Chapter Three

# Career Week

"Chloe, what is the topic for your presentation?" asked Mr. Mooney on Monday morning.

"Um, artist . . . um . . . lawyer . . . um . . . when do we have to finally decide?"

Mr. Mooney sighed. "I was hoping today. Last week's homework, remember? Think about what you might like to do when you finish school, talk it over with your parents, come in ready with your topic."

I nodded. "Sorry. Um . . . I thought I might do languages, but then I changed my mind and thought, no, I like art and . . . oh, I can't decide! But it's not my fault—I'm a Libran. My star sign can never decide."

"You're not the only one who knows about astrology, Chloe," said Mr. Mooney. "I am a Taurus, and we like to sit around watching TV and eating good food, but do I give in to it? No. I come to work and teach people like you. Do you see what I am saying? Sometimes you have to overcome some parts of your nature, so Libran or not, decide!"

*So much for sympathy*, I thought. All anyone was talking about was the eighth grade project. Last week had been a special "career week" with visiting speakers and talks at lunch. It was supposed to motivate us to start outlining a career path. We had to set goals, interview people in our chosen career, and even try to volunteer at that job. Then we had to present all that in front of the whole school. But even after career week I wasn't any closer to deciding, and I was getting bored of everyone being so into it, including Demi and Maryam, who were smug as bugs in rugs because they had chosen their topics weeks ago. I tried to keep an open mind and consider all the options, but I was beginning to think it was hopeless. I thought about choosing fashion designer with Maryam or a TV star, with lots of other options in between. Luckily Mr. Mooney shifted his attention from me.

"Well, who has chosen," he asked and looked hopefully around the class.

Janice Aitkin put up her hand. "An actress."

Sophie Smith put up hers. "Hairdresser, sir."

Barbara Reilley called out, "A teacher, sir." She got a nod of approval for that, but she's always been a teacher's pet.

Tracy Jones called out, "Interior designer."

Ellie Andrews, "A travel agent."

"I'm not going to work at all," said Susie Peterson. "I'm going to marry a millionaire."

Mr. Mooney rolled his eyes. "Good luck to you," he said.

I was thinking, *How can they know? How can they be so sure? Even "married to rich husband" is more than I can decide. Maybe I can fake it,* I thought. *No. Mr. Mooney is famous for failing kids who chose careers they don't really want.*

"And what about you?" Mr. Mooney asked Zoe Cain.

"Reality show celebrity," she replied.

Mr. Mooney sighed. "Reality show celebrity isn't a career choice, Zoe."

"Yes it is," Zoe said. "All you have to do is eat bugs or slugs in a remote jungle someplace or get locked up in a house for a few weeks or have a big boob job and you could be set for life."

Mr. Mooney sighed again, but the class laughed.

"Think again, Zoe," said Mr. Mooney. "And you, too, Susie Peterson."

I was glad I wasn't the only one who was being hassled for a plan. It was a difficult decision, a big choice, big pressure—what to do with the rest of our lives. Annoyingly, like the bridesmaid thing, everyone else seemed to be one step ahead of me. I've only ever wanted to be a bridesmaid, and that's not exactly a serious career choice.

*Hey, what about rock star?* I thought. When Mom walked into one of the meetings of the Bridesmaids' Club one month, she suggested that we start a band called the Bridesmaids. Sadly, even that turned out not to be a good idea because I'm tone deaf, Demi has the rhythm of a dead parrot, and although Maryam plays a musical instrument, it's the ukulele, which even I know isn't rock and roll.

While Mr. Mooney droned on, I reached down to my backpack and pulled out my zodiac phone. With all the fun of the fair, I hadn't had a chance to look at it much. I pressed the top to switch it on, and seconds later, it beeped loudly that there was a message. And another. Mr. Mooney swung around.

"Who's brought their phone to class?"

My desk is at the back of the room, and everyone turned around to look at me. Mr. Mooney marched down the aisle and put his hand out. "You know the rules, Bradbury. Give me the phone." I passed it over to him and he looked at it quizzically for a moment. Then he went to the front of the room and put it in the drawer of his desk. "You can have it back on Friday after school."

Uri's words "don't lose your phone," echoed in my mind. *Oops! So much for taking heed of his warning. How* was I supposed to know that Mr. Mooney would be on the warpath? But then again, Uri also said to expect the unexpected. Is this what he meant? Heck! I can't even contact him or Nessa to see what it's about. I put my forehead down on my desk and felt depressed for a few moments, and then I remembered that I still had Marcie's wedding to organize. You can't take that away from me, Mr. Mooney! I don't know what I want to be or do, but at least I have a wedding to look forward to!

## Chapter Four

# Surprise!

On the Sunday afternoon that Marcie was coming to visit, I got everything in my bedroom ready for her. I laid out fabric samples for dresses on the bed along with photos of a variety of designs by Nessa. I put the latest *Wedding* magazines in a pile on my desk. By the wall I propped up brochures showing various bouquets, one with roses, one with freesias, and one with white hyacinths. I had a ton of others to show her if she didn't go for what I'd put out on display.

My plan was that after the obligatory catch-up with Mom, I would make cups of hot chocolate for Marcie and me, and then we could escape up to my room and get on with the business at hand. As I busied myself putting out everything I'd collected from the wedding show, I felt a rush of excitement. *Life is just so wonderful,* I thought as I fished out a pile of leaflets about limos and horse-drawn carriages.

This year's wedding show had been the best so far, not only because of the new exhibits and getting the prize of being this month's Zodiac Girl, but also because I got to meet Nessa. I felt so happy as I remembered being the center of attention for those few minutes up on stage. Nessa had said something about being my guardian and about planet people being here to help me, and I realized later that she must mean that she and her colleagues would help me plan the perfect wedding. I guessed that being picked as a Zodiac Girl meant that I got the special promotions that were running for a month—I remembered Uri emphasizing something about the offer being good for four weeks only.

The zodiac phone was clearly a Celestial Weddings marketing ploy, too, because when I got it back from Mr. Mooney after school on Friday, I tried putting in numbers of my friends and family, but it didn't work. However, there were ten names and numbers in the address book already, all part of Celestial Weddings. Some of them I recognized from the fair, like Joe Joeve, Uri, and, of course, Nessa. *Very clever, to give out a phone with the names and numbers of all the aspects of the business. Much more imaginative than just using business cards,* I thought as I glanced over the list again.

1) Nessa: Venus
2) Sonny Olympus (Mr. O): Sun
3) Mario Ares: Mars

4) Hermie: Mercury
5) Joe Joeve: Jupiter
6) Captain John Dory: Neptune
7) Dr. Cronus: Saturn
8) Uri: Uranus
9) Selene Luna: Moon.
10) P. J.: Pluto.

*Yes, they are all definitely part of Celestial Weddings,* I decided, seeing as how they all had a planet after their name. If the quality of the rest of them was anything like Nessa's designs and Joe's fab food, we should hire the whole company.

The zodiac phone didn't work for phoning out either. I tried dialing Demi's number, but all I got was a voice telling me, "Number not listed in address book." I didn't mind too much because I already had a cell phone, and it worked fine although it wasn't as pretty. I gathered up the brochures about potential jobs that the lady doing career advice had given me and shoved them in my closet. Then I replaced them with lovely wedding mags. I still wasn't clear about what I wanted to do, but I wasn't going to worry about it today.

I heard the doorbell ring and raced downstairs, to find Marcie at the front door. She looked great, with a new haircut in soft layers around her face. I could just imagine it tied up with freesias wound into it, or maybe jasmine—the small star-shaped flowers would really stand out against her chestnut-colored hair. I'd let her decide.

"Congratulations!" I said and gave her a hug. She grinned and put her arms around me, and we did a little dance while still hugging.

Mom came out from the back room. She looks like an older version of Marcie, with the same dark hair and amber eyes. She joined in the hug. "Chloe's been researching your wedding while you've been away," she said when we pulled back. "I trust that you are still getting married? Haven't changed your mind on the plane back?"

*Always the same*, I thought. *Everyone in my family is doubtful that anything can ever work out.* I was about to say something but bit it back. I didn't want to ruin Marcie's good-news moment by arguing with Mom.

"No," said Marcie. "We've even fixed a date. June fifteenth, we thought."

I punched the air. "Yea! You'll be a summer bride. Fab. I've got loads of stuff to show you, Marce."

Marcie smiled, sort of—it was a cross between a smile and a wince. *Oh, poor thing*, I thought, *she's worried already. Everyone knows how stressful it is being a bride, but she has me. I will make it easy-peasy.*

"Lunch in five," Mom said. "Marcie, come and

chat while I set the table. How's Geoff? I thought you might have brought him along."

Marcie looked uncomfortable and shifted about from foot to foot. "Ah yes. Geoff. I have something to tell you about him."

We followed Mom into the kitchen, and Marcie sat at the table while Mom and I found silverware.

"Okay, I'm just going to come out and say it," Marcie blurted. "Um, Geoff. Yes. We broke up."

"You *what?*" I was horrified. "When?"

"A few weeks ago. Just before we were supposed to go to Paris."

"Before Paris?" I asked. "But you spoke to me. I don't understand. So the wedding's off?"

"Yes. No. I mean, yes, it's off with Geoff. I broke up with him before I went away."

Mom looked as puzzled as I was. "What about the engagement?" she asked. "What do you mean you broke up before you went away, Marcie, dear? You mean after, surely." Mom glanced at me. "She's clearly upset and has all her dates mixed up."

Marcie took a deep breath. "No, I haven't. I broke up with Geoff before I went away. Listen, he just wasn't right. That is, he was too right, he looked great, he was great, but . . . but . . . the chemistry wasn't there. I was going to tell you but . . . I knew that you all liked him and I didn't want you talking me out of it."

"But what about Paris? The proposal?" I asked. "You said June fifteenth for the wedding date when you came in."

Marcie nodded. "Yes. It is. And I did get engaged. That part is right."

"But you just said you broke up with Geoff," I said. "I'm confused."

"I did break up with Geoff. And I did get engaged. To Sam. I got engaged to Sam."

"Sam!" Mom and I chorused, and we both sat down with a thud.

Marcie nodded. "He got in touch a couple of nights before I went to Paris and begged me not to go. He said his life had been a misery without me, and just hearing his voice made me realize how much I'd missed him. I'd gone out with Geoff on the rebound, and it wasn't fair to keep stringing him along when I knew the magic ingredient wasn't there because all along I was still in love with Sam. I didn't think Sam would ever settle down, but he's changed and says he's realized that he can't live without me. As soon as I saw him, I knew in a second that all the old feelings were still there and, in fact, had never gone away."

"Sam?" I repeated. I couldn't take it in. Mom didn't seem too upset. She'd always liked Sam. She got up and finished setting the table and started serving lunch while she pressed Marcie for more details. I sat between them doing my goldfish impersonation. I was in shock as I listened. I couldn't get my head around it. Sam? *Sam?*

It turned out that Marcie never went to Paris. Instead Sam took her to a bed and breakfast in New Jersey. He proposed over breakfast. Hid the ring in a muffin. I couldn't help but feel disappointed. It was supposed to have been Paris, one of the most romantic cities in the world. There were so many fabulous locations that Sam could have chosen—a city in Spain or Italy, a beach in Morocco or even California, a balcony with a view, a sunset, a lovely moment to remember—not a breakfast table set with salt, pepper, maybe a ketchup bottle and a muffin in New Jersey. Sam? *Sam?* Pff! He had never struck me as someone who had much romance in his soul. Marcie was lucky he didn't give her the ring attached to a pair of sneakers.

"You okay, Chloe?" asked Marcie.

"Nff, yes, no. Just a bit of a shock, that's all. I . . . thought we were going to be welcoming Geoff into the family, and now, er . . . Are you absolutely sure, Marcie? I mean, you broke up with Sam."

"I have never been so sure about anything in my life. I love him. I always have. I broke up with him because he wouldn't make a commitment—you remember how he feels about weddings . . . But he told me that the months without me had been a complete misery and he'd do anything to have me back, even get married. I know he means it this time. I know he's The One."

I knew I shouldn't put a damper on her happiness, but my heart was sinking. *I can't let it show*, I thought. "Um. Tell me about the proposal again," I said.

She blushed slightly while she repeated the story, and she showed us her ring. Diamond. Classic. Not too flashy. *Kind of ordinary*, I thought. *A more modern design would have looked better*. But then Sam was a guy. A *guyish* guy. He couldn't be expected to keep up with the latest engagement jewelry.

"Are you quite quite *quite* sure?" I asked again.

"Chloe! Anyone would think that you're not happy for me. Don't you like Sam?" Marcie retorted.

"Um, yes, of course," I said. "He's . . . very handsome." He was. No denying that.

"He thinks you don't like him," said Marcie. "Please say you do, Chloe. For me. I know he made fun of the Bridesmaids' Club, but he's a real sweetie deep down. He wants you to like him, and I so want you to get along."

I didn't want to ruin her day. *I will do my best*, I thought, but looking at Marcie's finger and the ordinary ring made me more determined than ever to get the rest of the wedding right. "If you like him, then

I like him," I said in the most convincing way I could

I like him," I said in the most convincing way I could muster up. I didn't mention that I liked Geoff more.

After lunch was over and I washed the dishes, I finally managed to steal Marcie away.

"Wow! You've been busy," she said as she surveyed my room.

I pushed aside a pile of magazines to make space for her on my bed. "I have. I've already done a lot of sifting through and eliminated a lot of the cliché or boring stuff, so we only have the best ideas to look at. I met the most *amazing* new people at the fair. I think we should hire all of them."

Again a worried expression crossed Marcie's face. Not so much a smile as a wince. I took her hand. "Hey, it's going to be all right. If you think that Sam is the right man for you, then I will do my best to get along better with him. You're going to have a perfect wedding, don't you worry." I meant it, too—I'd compromise on the groom as long as I got my chance to be a bridesmaid.

"Thanks, Chloe, and of course I will look at what you've picked out. It's just . . . well . . . Sam and I talked about it when we were away . . ."

I passed her the first bunch of brochures to look at. "Great," I said. "It's always good to get input from the groom. We want everyone to be happy."

She reached into the pocket of her jeans and pulled

out a slip of paper. "Well," she said. "You know that Sam thinks weddings are basically about a piece of paper, so I agreed to compromise on the ceremony and have some . . . er, fun. We decided, or, that is, these are mainly Sam's ideas, they are . . . um . . . a bit different."

I took the piece of paper. "Good. Different is good. We don't want your wedding to be like any other, and I am sure it won't be. Oh, Marcie, I have met the most awesome woman. She does dresses and makeup and . . ." I glanced at the list and did a double take. I read it again and laughed. "Oh, very good, Marcie. Very funny. You almost got me there for a moment." I sat down next to her. "And how long have you been planning this little joke?"

Marcie wasn't laughing. "Not a joke. It will be fun but I'm serious about it. We want our wedding to be a day to remember, and Sam thought if we picked something on this list, it would be."

I looked back at the list. Sam's wedding suggestions were as follows:

1) Roller-skate wedding
2) Velcro wedding
3) Bungee-jump wedding
4) Underwater wedding
5) Bridezilla wedding (with bride and groom dressed as gorillas)

*Oh. My. God!* I thought as my mind filled with horror. It couldn't be true. "You're really serious?"

Marcie nodded. "Serious."

"But these ideas are weird. Crazy," I said. I glanced back down at the list. *Sam's input?* I thought. *What about my input? Years of it. But no, Sam is the groom. He gets his say. Oh Geoff, come back. Where are you?* I glanced up at Marcie again and wished that she loved him, not Sam. "What what about all the work I've done? I've been planning this for years!"

A flash of irritation crossed Marcie's face. She stood up and her cheeks flushed pink. "My wedding, Chloe. *My* wedding. Mine and Sam's, so we have first say. You could have at least tried to understand but no, you just want it your way. You aren't happy that the man I love has asked me to marry him, and you can't hide it." She looked close to tears as she stood up and went to the door, where she turned back to look at me. "You are the most selfish person, Chloe, and you're only thinking of yourself and what you want in all of this."

She went out and slammed the door behind her. I was stunned. Marcie never lost it. Jane and Clare, yes, but not Marcie. I heard her stomp down the stairs and then the front door banged shut. I lay back on my bed and burst into tears. It wasn't fair. I had just wanted the wedding plans to be nice for everyone—that wasn't selfish. How could she accuse me of that? I only wanted everything to be beautiful for her. Oh, rotten bananas! *Am I feeling bad because I want my own way?* I wondered. *This is so not how it was meant to be.*

# Chapter Five

# Arghhhh!

After Marcie left, I picked up Sergeant Ted, my favorite teddy bear, from his place on my bed, cuddled up to him, and then sat and stared at the phone. I wanted to call Demi or Maryam and tell them the awful news about Marcie marrying Sam and their crazy wedding plans, but I wasn't ready for their reaction. They were bound to laugh because the whole idea was ridiculous.

I put away my bridesmaid album and stacked all the magazines and brochures and tossed them in the bottom of the closet next to the boring career leaflets, and then stared out the window. I felt shocked. Numb. Not a single one of the options on Marcie's list had featured in my album. Not *one*. I felt like lying on the floor and having a temper tantrum like a three-year-old. *I planned for everything except this*, I said to myself. A sound like wind chimes rang out, and my zodiac phone began to vibrate and slide around on my bureau until it fell onto the carpet. I picked it up and pressed a green button that was flashing.

"All right, Chloe," said Nessa. "Nessa here."

"Oh, hi, Nessa," I said. "So it does work."

"What? The phone? Course. It's for you and me to stay in touch. I've been looking at your chart, and there's a lot going on for you at the moment, unsettling stuff. I thought you might have called."

"Chart? Called you? About the wedding?"

"No. Because you're our Zodiac Girl this month and I'm here to help."

"I couldn't call even if I'd thought of it. One of my teachers confiscated my phone last Monday and I only got it back on Friday night, and anyway, I didn't think I could call out on it."

I could hear Nessa tsk. "Course, Mercury was retrograde—that always messes up communications. Unfortunate when that happens in a Zodiac Girl's month—it means we can't always reach you. We never know exactly how Mercury's goin' retrograde is going to manifest—sometimes computers break down, Internet access gets lost, phone batteries die, that sort of thing. And with you, your teacher took your phone. But at least it was only for a week and now we're back on track. Ah well, what's done is done. You'll get other opportunities."

I had no idea what Nessa was talking about.

"Opportunities? To do what?" I asked.

"To be your very best self. To be who you're meant to be."

Her words made me feel more depressed than ever. Be who I'm meant to be? That was my other problem. "And that's another thing, Nessa. At school we are supposed to give a huge presentation about what we want to do when we're older, and I don't have a clue! I don't know what I want to do or who I want to be. Life stinks. I keep changing my mind about everything."

"Your chart said you had a difficult time ahead. Neptune, that's the planet of dreams, crossed by Pluto and Saturn. Tough going, doll."

"Are they two more of your colleagues in the wedding business?"

"Yes, but they're also planets in your chart, and they're set against each other at a difficult angle."

"I don't know much about astrology, Nessa. In fact, I don't know what you mean at all."

"Saturn is the taskmaster of the zodiac. When he's crossed or at a difficult angle in your chart, it means there's a lesson to be learned. Pluto is the planet of transformation. He can descend to the roots of your ideas and shake them up. Put those two at a tricky angle with Neptune—"

"The planet of dreams."

"That's it. You're getting it. Put those three

together, and I'd say that some dream of yours has been shaken or shattered."

I still wasn't sure what she was talking about and why she had to bring planets into it all the time, but maybe that was her thing, her way of expressing herself. Whatever—she seemed to have grasped that things had gone wrong. "Tell me about it. Shaken *and* shattered, Nessa. And not some dream—my *life's* dream."

"Didn't you get my text?"

"Yes. Um, not to resist or something."

"Exactly," said Nessa. "Listen, darlin', you have to ride out this next bit of your life like you're surfin' a wave. Yeah, it's a tidal wave, but don't fight what's happenin'. You gotta go with the flow."

"But, Nessa, everything's gone wrong and now my sister hates me."

"Why? What's happened?"

"My sister Marcie is getting married to an idiot who thinks that weddings are a joke. He's going to ruin theirs and I'm going to be the laughing stock of the school. I had it all planned and wanted to use your designs and your friends in the planet company, too, but I am sorry, it's not going to happen."

"Hey, I'm not here to sell you Celestial Weddings," said Nessa. "I'm here to help."

*That's sweet*, I thought and I blinked back a tear.

"Okay. Listen to this then." I read Marcie's list. I heard a soft laugh at the other end.

"See? I *knew* people would laugh, and I don't blame you. And now I know I can't ever tell my friends. Marcie didn't even look at half the stuff I had laid out for her, and now she hates me and thinks I'm selfish, which is so not fair because all I have been doing these past few weeks is thinking about her."

"Chloe, darlin', this is part of what being a Zodiac Girl is about. It's a time of transition, of growth. And sometimes growth is painful and confusin'. But, honey, you're in great company. Some of the most famous women in history were Zodiac Girls. Marie Curie, Cleopatra, Elizabeth the First—she was one but . . . Are you cryin', doll?"

"No."

"Chloe. Chloe. Listen, darlin'. Help is at hand."

"Nothing could help. Not unless you know Marcie or Sam and can talk them out of this stupid plan."

"This isn't about them. It's about *you*. You. You're at a turning point in your life. It's not always clear at first why a girl has been chosen to be Zodiac Girl, and it's really up to you to make of it what you will. What we have to figure out is why you've been chosen and what you're supposed to get out of it. I think this big letdown of yours is part of it. It may not be as bad as you think."

"My sister dressed as a gorilla or bungee jumping instead of floating down the aisle in one of your beautiful creations! How much worse could it get?"

Nessa laughed again. "Yeah. Not quite your dreamy, gorgeous wedding. But remember that nothin' is set in stone. Want to know one of my favorite sayings?"

I was feeling so miserable that I didn't really want to hear cute sayings, but I knew it would be rude not to say yes. "Yes. What is it? Darkest hour is just before dawn?"

"No. Although that is a good one. My favorite saying is, 'What you resist, persists.' It's a good lesson in life, Chloe, if you really get it. What I am sayin' is, go along with your sister's plans. Try not to resist. In fact, try to enjoy the process. It just so happens that Celestial Weddings offers alternative weddings as well as traditional ones. You could come have a look for free during your school vacation next week. We could check out a different option on the list each day. Could be fun."

*Fun?* I thought. *Are you kidding?*

"Your sister needs to explore her options," said Nessa.

"These aren't options, they're catastrophes," I groaned as I threw the list into the wastebasket.

"Remember that saying—that's all I'm goin' to ask for now. What you resist, persists, so go along with your sister and *enjoy* it."

I liked Nessa and I wanted her to like me so I decided to agree. "Okay. Maybe."

"Good girl. We'll be in touch. *Nil desperandum.*"

"Yeah, right. Nil desperwhatsit. Whatever."

Nessa laughed and then hung up. I picked the list out of the wastebasket and glanced at it again. *What can I do?* I asked myself. *Stamp my foot like a spoiled princess, cry myself sick and force Marcie to do what I want no matter what? That isn't an option, either.*

I got up and kicked the wall. "Ow! That hurt!" I groaned as my toe throbbed big time. "But . . . *Arghhhh!* Life stinks sometimes," I said to Sergeant Ted. "It's so hard when the one thing you've always wanted doesn't turn out the way you expect. Is this how it's going to be from now on? Letdown after letdown? Will I spend my entire life staggering from one disappointment to another? Will *nothing* turn out as planned?"

Sergeant Ted didn't reply. He's a bear of few words.

"Don't look at me like that," I said to him. "I know, I know. Nessa was right. I'll call Marcie and say that I'll give it a try, okay?"

I swear Sergeant Ted nodded at the same time as my zodiac phone beeped that I had a message, then another, then another.

One was from Nessa:

Uranus is square to Mars and Saturn in your chart and at a tricky angle to Neptune and Pluto. I said it was going to be a difficult time! However, Venus is conjunct with Mercury at a favorable angle, so there will be a bit of a reprieve, and a harmonious time is coming up, too, probably tomorrow.

*She was right about the difficult time,* I thought as I checked the second message, which was from Uri. He had written:

A friend is someone who knows your secret dream and holds your hand when it shatters.

On a good day I might have thought his words were way sappy, like, *blurgh,* vomit, but at that moment, they touched me. *That's so true,* I thought. I always shared everything with Maryam and Demi, good and bad. We had always been there for each other— like when Maryam's dad was ill last summer and she was so upset, and last semester when Demi liked a boy in the ninth grade and he went off with Tania Cosgrave and Demi was gutted. We had always sworn to be there for each other. I shouldn't cut them out now just because I was afraid they might laugh. *Right on, Uri,* I thought. *Friends are for rain and shine.*

The third message was from Nessa again, and it said:

**The Sun is well aspected to Mercury next week. Enjoy.**

*More planet gobbledegook. Nessa really is into it,* I thought as I picked up my normal cell phone to send a text to Demi and Maryam. All it said was **SOS**. That was our code for *help needed and fast*. Dad had told me ages ago that "SOS" was sent out by ships if they were in danger, and if anyone received the message, they would send back "WILCO," which means *Got your message and will comply*.

Two minutes after I had sent the message, I got two texts back saying **WILCO**.

Twenty minutes later, Maryam and Demi were at the door with a bag of jelly beans and a bottle of root beer (both my all-time faves).

# Chapter Six

# Option One

"You ready?" Marcie called up the stairs.

"Coming," I called back from my bedroom, where I had been getting ready with Demi and Maryam. It was a freezing day outside, cold, gray, and misty, and I had pulled out all the scarves, gloves, and woolly hat sets that my grandma had knitted for me over the years and put them on the bed for my friends to wear. Maryam had chosen a turquoise set, mine was pink, and Demi's was scarlet. We were about to leave when I changed my mind and thought that maybe pale blue would be nicer for today.

Demi took the blue one and shoved it back in my drawer. "Pink. Pink. *Pink!* If we wait for you to decide, we'll be here all day. You know what you're like."

I let her boss me around sometimes because she was right. Some days I would agonize over the smallest decisions. We all stood in the model pose that we had learned from one of Demi's fashion mags—

body turned left side forward, with left hip dropped, shoulders and head facing forward—then checked our reflections in the mirror. "We may only be going roller skating," I said in a silly English accent, "but we should *never* forget our sense of style."

We did our club's sign to each other, left thumbs up, down, up, then jostled each other out into the hall and downstairs to meet Marcie.

"And so school vacation begins," she said as she ushered us out the door and into her Volkswagen.

"So how does this roller-skating wedding thing work?" asked Demi once we were in the back of the car and on our way. I did love her and Maryam. They'd been great when I broke the news to them about Marcie's list, and they hadn't laughed, at least not until I got to the Bridezilla option, when they did crack up for a few seconds. They had understood right away how upset I was and had done their best to cheer me up. As members of the Bridesmaids' Club, both of them insisted on coming with me to research the list, and somehow it didn't seem so depressing knowing that they would be there, especially for the roller skating. I am horrible at it—have been ever since I was seven and got a pair of skates for Christmas and our dog, Boris, was more excited by them than I was. Every time I got my balance and skated off, he'd run after me, jump up, and flatten me. Over and over again. Being bruised and battered again as a bridesmaid didn't hold much appeal, but I think Marcie had conveniently forgotten about my earlier disasters. She was so happy when I called late last night and said I'd be willing to try out her list with her.

"The idea is that the ceremony is conducted by a minister on skates in a park in the center of town. The bride, the groom, and the guests strap on skates and skate along behind him to that lovely gazebo by the fountain."

"What, even Grandma?" I asked. "No way will she be able to skate."

"Oh no! You're right," Marcie replied. "I hadn't thought of how the older guests would skate. Okay, so maybe just a few of us can do the skating thing."

*One point against,* I tallied mentally when I saw a flicker of doubt register on Marcie's face. *Maybe this isn't going to be as hard as I thought!*

"I think you should give people the choice," I said. "I mean, not everyone, no matter what their age, can skate. Remember Boris?"

"Boris?"

"Yes. Boris. Our dog. Remember when I was little? He jumped up whenever I put skates on and sent me flying over and over again. I will give it a try today, but I am not very good at it."

"Oh Chloe! I am so sorry. I had completely forgotten about that. Um . . . you don't have to do it if you don't want to. In fact, maybe it should just be me and Sam and the minister." Marcie looked even more worried.

*Two points against,* I thought. *This is going to be so easy. Nessa was right. Don't resist and things may work out after all.*

"How did you know that Sam was The One and not Geoff?" Demi asked.

"Oh, the way I feel when I'm with him," Marcie replied. "Kind of tingly all over, light-headed—"

"That's how I feel when I get the flu," I interrupted, and Demi and Maryam cracked up. "Sorry, Marcie—couldn't resist. But surely it must be more than that?"

"If you'd let me finish!" said Marcie, but she was smiling so I knew she didn't mind being teased. "I feel comfortable with him, more comfortable than with any other man I've been out with, and I can't wait to see him again. I love spending time with him. Geoff was a nice guy, maybe too nice—but the spark just wasn't there the way it is with Sam."

"So how come he's managed to bully you into trying out all these wacky weddings, Marcie? I just don't get it. When you were younger you always planned to have a traditional wedding. What's made you change your mind?"

"I . . . uh . . . A relationship is about compromise, Chloe. About listening to the other person's point of view. About sharing."

"But he's left you to check out all the wedding options by yourself," I said. "Why isn't he here sharing this?"

"My mom says you have to start a marriage the way you intend to continue," added Demi, "and that's by sharing the chores."

"Did you tell him that you wanted a traditional wedding?" asked Maryam.

"Not exactly," said Marcie. Then she was quiet for a while. "And he couldn't get out of his commitments this week—he had to take a group of students hiking, and he had just taken the week off to be with me," she said finally, but for the rest of the way to the park, she looked reflective, and I wondered if our comments had touched a nerve.

When we got to the park, Marcie stopped the car and we got out and looked around for the skating representative, but all we saw were a woman walking her dog and a man eating a sandwich on a bench.

"She said she'd meet us here," said Marcie.

"At least it's stopped misting," Demi commented as she looked around at the damp grass.

"Is that her?" asked Maryam as a large woman in a

violet sweatsuit came roller-blading (or, rather, roller-blundering) down the path toward us.

"Omigod!" I heard Marcie say under her breath. The woman was clearly was not a natural on skates, she and huffed and puffed to keep her balance. I glanced at Demi and Maryam, who had fixed bright expressions on their faces. I could tell that they were dying to laugh. *Whew!* I thought as she skated past. *Not her.*

I shot Demi and Maryam another glance. Demi raised her right eyebrow. I knew we were all thinking the same thing—that the whole idea of a roller-skate wedding was tack city.

Then he came out of nowhere. A flash of silver against the gray morning, a skater flying by as if he had winged feet.

"Wow!" we chorused as the silver blur turned and skated back toward us, slowing down as he approached.

"Double wow!" said Demi.

"Triple that," said Maryam.

The skater was a total babe. Tall and athletic, he was dressed in a silver padded jumpsuit, the kind that people wear to go skiing, and he had shoulder-length brown wavy hair. It was hard to tell how old he was, maybe eighteen, but his eyes looked older, wiser, as though he had seen something of life. He had perfect skin, a square jaw, and cheekbones to die for, and I felt my knees turn to jelly as he bowed, flashed us a killer smile, did a quick spin on his skates, and took off his backpack.

"Hi, I'm Hermie."

"Nuf, ki . . . yeah," I stuttered.

"Kee, yud, ee," said Demi.

"Yom," said Maryam.

"Werd . . ." said Marcie.

I giggled. We all seemed to be suffering from the same lack of mouth-to-brain coordination. Hermie smiled. He was probably used to girls falling apart in front of him.

"I'm part of the Celestial Weddings company," he said. "I'm waiting for my partner. She'll be here soon. Want to try out while we wait?"

"Yes!" we chorused. Even I was excited now. Hermie reached into his backpack and pulled out four pairs of silver skates, which he handed out. We sat down on a bench and put them on—they all fit perfectly, although I didn't remember telling anyone our sizes. Demi and Maryam were both blushing and stealing glances at Hermie. When we had our skates on, he skated in front of Marcie and held out his hands to her. She reached for him, and he pulled her up, let go, and off she went. Next Hermie helped

Demi, then Maryam, and they skated off, too. I fiddled with my laces.

"Ready?" asked the most gorgeous boy in the world.

"Um, I'm not very good at skating."

"Bad experience when you were little, huh?"

"How did you know?"

"It was in your birth chart. When you were about seven?"

"But . . . huh . . . how did you know?"

"I'm a friend of Nessa's. You're the Zodiac Girl, right?"

"Yes. Although I'm not completely sure what that means."

Hermie held his hands out to me. "It means be brave! Have the time of your life. Come on. Give it a try."

I really wanted him to like me and I didn't want him to think I was a coward, so when he grasped my hands I wobbled to my feet. Once I was sort of upright, he gave me a little shove and then skated off to check on the others. I skated along as best as I could, holding on to the backs of park benches, trash cans—whatever I could hang on to. Suddenly the path became a downhill slope. I could see Hermie and the others glide down, slowing gradually as the path became level again at the bottom. I took a deep breath and started down the hill. Not good! I lost control completely and sped toward a duck pond, wailing my head off.

"WARGHHH! Help!"

Hermie raced to my rescue, grabbed my waist, and slowed me down to a speed that was slightly less terrifying.

"Don't let go," I panted.

"I won't," he said, and he took my hands and skated backward while I skated forward.

"Okay?" he asked.

"Wurgh." It took a moment but I realized that I was skating really well. "Actually, yeah! But don't let go yet."

"I promise I won't. Now relax. Take three deep breaths. In, blow out. In, blow out. In, blow out."

I did as I was told and felt a bit better.

"So, Zodiac Girl. What do you know about astrology?" asked Hermie.

"Not much. I'm a Libran. Demi's a Gemini. Maryam's a Sagittarius. I know a bit about Librans now—like we're lovers of beauty, um . . . don't like being rushed . . ."

"Which is probably why roller-skating wasn't your favorite thing," said Hermie. "But you're doing very well and relaxing into it. Did you know that each sign has a ruling planet?"

"Sort of. Nessa said something about it."

"Librans are ruled by Venus. That's Nessa. I'm Mercury, the planet of communication, which rules Virgo and Gemini."

"I saw that all the branches of Celestial Weddings are named after planets. I think that's so cool."

Hermie looked at me intently, then he sighed. "Anyway. Did you know that Mercury is also known as the winged messenger?"

"No, but that's a good name for you. You skate as if you have winged feet."

Hermie laughed. "My thing is mainly communication. Nessa told me that you were freaked out about your sister's wedding plans."

"They did come out of the blue."

"That would be because Uranus is in your chart. He brings the unexpected, like a bolt of lightning."

"Exactly."

"But you're coping well. That's because essentially Libra is an easygoing sign—"

"Yes, and I hate it when people don't get along."

"What I'd like to communicate to you," Hermie continued, "is that you need to try to see both sides. Think you can do that? Should be easy for a Libran."

"See that my ideas were fab and hers are insane?" I asked. "Easy."

Hermie laughed and shook his gorgeous mane of

hair as we glided along at a gentle pace. "All you have to do is let go. Think of your month as a Zodiac Girl as an adventure and enjoy the ride."

I had to admit that skating with Hermie was quite enjoyable. I let go of him, and then it felt amazing, like I was floating. I dared to glance to my side and saw that Demi, Marcie, and Maryam were doing really well, all confident skaters. We skated to the end of the path and stopped.

"Oh, here comes Nessa," said Hermie. He pointed to the top of the hill. I turned, and at that moment the clouds parted and a ray of sun shone down like a spotlight on the part of the path where Nessa stood, resplendent in a beautiful white skating outfit trimmed with fake fur, her hair wound into a delicate crown that looked as if it was made from icicles. She looked every inch a snow queen, and I was mesmerized. She skated down to join Hermie, and together they continued along the path. They were totally in step with each other, graceful and elegant. To their left I could see that Demi, Maryam, and Marcie had stopped skating and, like me, were watching the performance. An image began to form in my mind despite all my former resistance: Marcie in a similar outfit trimmed with crystals, a tiara on her head. She'd glide to the outdoor altar. Sam in black beside her. Behind them, Demi, Maryam, and me in tiny silver skirts like cheerleaders. We could even put together a skating routine. It didn't have to be tacky at all. It could be the talk of the year. "So innovative. So daring," the guests would say. I'd certainly never seen anything like it in any of the wedding magazines. We could be the first. Could it be a possibility? *No, no*, I thought, *I mustn't let myself be persuaded.*

Nessa must have picked up on my thoughts because she skated over to me.

"Could be lovely, couldn't it?" she asked.

"Maybe."

"Everything in life is what you make of it. Harmony or disaster, it's your choice."

I was about to tell her that my choice would still be a traditional wedding with Marcie as a classic beautiful bride, when the woman in the purple sweats who had clumsily skated past earlier came huffing along the path. She looked Nessa and Hermie up and down with disapproval. "Lesson number one, my dears," she barked. "Outfits like that won't do, you know. You'll catch your death. Heavy sweaters, that's what you need." And with that, she skated off again, leaving us trying not to laugh.

Marcie skated to a stop behind us. "Thank you so much," she said to Hermie and Nessa. "All very impressive."

Even though they'd made it look lovely, I wasn't going to let myself be convinced that easily.

In the car going home, I gave the matter some serious thought. A wedding on roller skates wasn't what I wanted for Marcie or myself, not by a long shot, but maybe it wasn't as bad as I had first imagined. "If you do go for it," I said, "we'd better have a covered aisle in case it rains, and we have to make it clear that the older people don't have to skate."

"Yes, of course," said Marcie. "And it was fun, wasn't it?"

"Sort of," I said.

"I think it could be great," said Demi. "We just need to make sure we have the right outfits. Something like Hermie and Nessa were wearing."

"Exactly," said Maryam. "Cutie cute."

Marcie looked thoughtful. "Yes, but it's only option one. We still have other ideas to try, and you may have been right in the beginning, Chloe. It might be risky, and I don't want a wedding where we have to call in the paramedics to stitch up someone's knee."

"Calling in the paramedics doesn't have to be a problem," said Demi. "They could be on skates, too. It could be a whole production. Hermie and Nessa could be on the guest list, too, in case you need any skating backup."

"I guess," said Marcie, but I could see that she was worried about broken bones and elderly aunts and uncles. By the time we got home, I got the feeling that option one might be struck from the list.

# Chapter Seven

# Velcro!

"So what's number two on the list?" I asked when I got into the car the next morning. I'd bundled up warm because once again the day was wet and gray. This time, it was just Marcie and me because Maryam and Demi had both been hauled off to spend "quality" time with their families. None of us was crazy about "quality" time because it usually involved listening to a lecture of some sort about homework or bad behavior or, in my case, what topic I should choose for my eighth grade project. I still didn't know despite spending hours browsing the career options brochures last night before I went to bed.

Marcie's worries seemed to have evaporated over-night, and she was in a positive mood again. "I think this one is going to be great," she said. "It's the Incredible Velcro wedding. I'm not sure what happens exactly."

"Their slogan could be 'You'll be stuck for life,'" I joked.

Marcie laughed. "Oh, very good. And, Chloe, I want you to know that I do appreciate your coming with me. I know Sam would have liked to come with us, but as you know, he had things to do, so it's up to me and thee. Just like old times, huh? I know it's not what you had in mind for me, but I think it's fantastic that you are willing to give it a try."

I wasn't sure if it was wishful thinking on my part, but I thought I detected a hint of regret when she said that it wasn't what I had in mind for her. Maybe there was room for persuasion to bring her back to her senses at a later date. Today I was following Nessa's and Hermie's advice and taking the path of least resistance, trying to see it as an adventure and enjoy it.

Nessa had called just before we set out and said that she might see me later—something to do with Uranus and Venus in my chart. Uranus was Uri. I was beginning to get the hang of her colleagues in the wedding business and their nicknames. All I had to do was look on my zodiac phone to see their listings. Hermie was down as Mercury, Nessa as Venus, Uri, Uranus—I explained it all to Marcie, and, like me, she thought it was a great marketing concept.

She followed the directions to the Velcro wedding center, and after a short drive we ended up in what looked like an industrial park. I felt my heart sink—it was the most unglamorous location I had ever seen. No trees, just concrete buildings covered in graffiti, warehouses with broken windows, a former carpet store that was now empty and boarded up. And that was it. Definitely not a place to bring a wedding party.

"Are you sure you have the right place?" I asked as I got out of the car and pulled my jacket tight around me. I didn't like the look of the location at all—it had a menacing feel about it, and the enthusiasm I'd mustered the previous day was fast disappearing. *Roller-skating with a babe like Hermie, maybe*, I thought. *Getting married in Velcro, I am not so sure.*

"I'm supposed to call a number when we arrive," said Marcie, looking at a slip of paper, "and someone will come out to meet us."

"Does Mom know that we're here?" I asked as I noticed dark alleys at the sides of the buildings and a pile of broken bottles and trash blowing around in the wind.

Marcie laughed. "Why? Do you think we might disappear?"

I nodded and Marcie laughed again but her laughter was hollow. I could see that she didn't like the place any more than I did. A gust of wind sent wrappers and papers into the air. I had a bad feeling. "Let's go home," I suggested.

Marcie nodded, and we were about to get into the

car when a dark figure appeared in the alley. My heart leaped into my mouth as the figure began to approach us. "Quick," I said to Marcie. "Someone's there."

We scrambled into the car, and Marcie locked the doors and started the engine. The man in the shadows came into view. He was tall and thin and dressed from head to toe in black. He came over to the car and Marcie opened the window a crack.

"You come for the Velcro wedding?" he asked, revealing an uneven set of yellow teeth.

Marcie nodded.

"Come on then, you're late," said the man. "I'm Don Waters, the guide—at least for now." He beckoned us to follow him and headed toward the warehouse. I noticed that he walked with a slight limp.

"We'd better go with him," said Marcie, "in case there's some kind of cancellation fee."

"But I can already tell that this will be a no without us even having to go in. Can't you?" I said as we got out of the car.

"We can cut it short and then take off," Marcie agreed.

Don led us down the alley, through a side door, and then into a dark corridor. He flipped a switch and a fluorescent light flickered weakly overhead. I glanced up and saw a bulb so covered in dust and cobwebs that it barely gave off any light. Don then opened a door, and we found ourselves in the vast open space of the warehouse. He switched on another light, and in the corner I saw an enormous trampoline. Don pointed at it. "That's where you'll be. I'll tell you what to do, but I don't do it myself anymore." He indicated his leg. "Your costumes are in there," he continued, and he pointed at a shabby-looking door with a piece of paper stuck on it on which someone had written "DRESING RuM." Inside, there was a smell of must and stale sweat. Marcie looked at the Velcro costumes that were hanging on a rail. She wrinkled her nose.

"This place is horrible, Marcie. Do we have to do this?" I asked. "Can't you say you're not feeling well?"

Marcie hesitated. "Um . . . yes. Sam, my love, this is going too far. There are some things that I am willing to do for love, but putting on a smelly old Velcro outfit in this stinky dark hole of a place is asking too much and is not my idea of fun."

"I agree," I said. "I can't believe he would put you through this."

Feeling hugely relieved, I followed her back into the main room, where, to my surprise, I saw Nessa and Uri had arrived. They were handing over what looked like a huge wad of cash to Don, who was looking gleeful.

Nessa saw us and waved us over.

"I'll be off, then. These idiots . . . I mean these folks will show you the ropes," said Don, and with a yellow grin at us, he limped off.

I introduced Marcie to Uri.

"Dressed for the part, I see," I said. Uri had on an electric blue jumpsuit with black lightning flashes up the sides, and his white-blond hair was spiked up like he had a ton of gel in it. Nessa was wearing a pale pink sweatsuit that looked like it might be made of Velcro.

Uri grinned. "Something like that. Are you ready for the Velcro experience, Marcie?"

"Yes, but we're not sure, I mean, maybe another day. We were just about to leave, in fact."

"First time, huh?" asked Uri.

We both nodded.

"Well, you've come all this way—at least give it one try," he said. "You'll have a blast. Now, let me see if I can get my lights working." He picked up a box, went to the wall, and plugged in what looked like a slide projector. Immediately the room was flooded with lights, and not just any lights—it was a laser show with swirling lightning flashes, stars, and fireworks. The display magically transformed the place. It no longer looked spooky at all.

"Over here, girls," said Nessa. Out of a bag that she had brought with her, she produced two pale pink sweatsuits like the one she was wearing. "Pure Velcro," she said as she held them up to us. "I've been researchin' the material, and it doesn't have to look yucky. If you go for the Velcro wedding, you can decide on the design details and so on at a later date."

I took one, and the material felt soft and smelled wonderful, like it had been washed and hung out to dry in the fresh air.

"Shall we, Marcie? At least give it a try?" I asked.

She glanced up at the trampoline and then at me. Then she grinned, and I got a glimpse of the old fun Marcie. "Why not?"

We slipped into the DRESING RuM. I got ready right away. Marcie was taking forever fixing her hair, so I went out to join Uri.

"Wow! What happened?" I asked. The light show had been turned off, and Nessa was busy mopping. I had only been gone about five minutes, but the space looked immaculate, as if it had been given a coat of paint. What's more it smelled divine, like fresh flowers. "It's as if you waved a magic wand. How did you clean up so fast, Nessa?"

Nessa smiled and tapped the side of her nose. "Maybe I can work a bit of magic here and there when it's needed. I hate a messy room, don't you? I like everythin' to be beautiful and harmonious. I get upset otherwise."

"Yes, me too, but how did you do it?" I asked again. I took a long look at her and a crazy thought occurred to me. Maybe she was an angel or a fairy godmother. Maybe she really *was* able to do magic.

"I can move fast when I need to as well," she said, and then she turned and went over toward the trampoline in the corner. "Now help me up on that, please. Give me five minutes to dust off the surface, and then up you come." She started to climb up, and Uri came over to join me.

"So how's the Zodiac Girl time going?" he asked. "This is your second week in, isn't it? Nessa said you missed our help the first week, but that wasn't surprising seeing as Mercury was retrograde."

"Mercury—that's Hermie's business, isn't it?"

"Not his business. Hermie *is* Mercury."

I felt confused. "And retrograde—that means going backward, doesn't it?"

Uri nodded.

"What, like skating backward?"

Uri laughed. "No. When Mercury is retrograde, which happens a few times a year, it means that all sorts of things can go wrong with communications."

"My teacher confiscated my phone."

"A perfect example. It's just a shame that it fell in your Zodiac Girl month."

Sometimes I found the people in the Celestial Weddings company had a strange way of communicating. Planets, retrograde, zodiacs—why couldn't they just say what they meant? I decided to try and put it in plain language for him.

"I know that the promotion is for a month, and Nessa has given me some good advice. She said to let go and enjoy this week, and that's what I'm trying to do."

"That *is* good advice. In fact, the only way to do it. Go with the flow—that's another way of saying it."

"It was hard to feel enthusiastic when we got here earlier and saw what a dump this place was. I can't imagine why you'd want to add Velcro weddings to your company's list of options. And there's a whole list of other names in my zodiac phone address book. Where do they come into it? Are they all in the Celestial Weddings business, too?"

Uri sprang back and did a cartwheel across the warehouse floor, then somersaulted back. "The others will introduce themselves, but only if they're prevalent in your chart this month. Not every Zodiac Girl meets all ten of us."

"Why are *you* in the wedding business, Uri?"

"For you. We adapt ourselves to the needs of our Zodiac Girl."

I felt that he was talking in riddles, but then it didn't surprise me—he looked like the kind of person who would do that.

"For me, huh?"

Uri nodded. "Ten planets. Each sign has a ruling planet."

*Here he goes again*, I thought. "I know, and Venus rules Libra, but I thought there were twelve birth signs, so why only ten ruling planets?" I was sure I'd read about the twelve signs in one of my mags.

Uri nodded again. "Libra and Taurus share Venus as their ruling planet. And Gemini and Virgo share Mercury as theirs. All the other signs have their own planet. Aries is ruled by Mars, Cancer by the Moon, Leo by the Sun, Pisces by Neptune, Capricorn by Saturn, Scorpio by Pluto, Sagittarius by Jupiter, and Aquarius by Uranus."

I decided to try and talk to Uri in his own strange language. "Uri, I hate to say this but . . . I think you might be retrograde because . . . don't be offended, but I think you have a problem with the way you communicate. You need to speak more directly."

Uri burst out laughing like I'd made the best joke ever.

"What's so funny?" I asked.

"You are," he replied. "Each Zodiac Girl makes sense of what's happening to her in her own individual way but . . . I have never come across anyone like you before. You . . . you're amazing. One of a kind."

"Thanks," I said, although I wasn't sure if he was paying me a compliment or not. *This is a lesson in life*, I decided. *Sometimes I won't have a clue what some people are going on about. And that's okay.* "Now, try again, Uri. Try again to explain about you and the wedding business, but try to keep it simple."

Uri looked as if he might start laughing again. "Okay. So where was I? Right. Uranus is the planet of rebellion. Some people say it's the planet of eccentricity, certainly the unexpected. So my part in the wedding scene is anything that is off the beaten path, like a Velcro wedding. If you'd looked at your chart, you would have seen that Uranus has a strong influence at this time, hence my telling you to expect the unexpected."

"It's been that all right. First Marcie's list and now this. But I don't understand any of it. I thought I was a Libran, and that's ruled by Venus, but now you're saying Uranus is an influence?"

"All the planets have some influence on a person's chart at some time or other depending on when you were born. Have you looked at the horoscope that I gave you?"

"Um, not really. That is, I did take a quick peek, but it looked like a graph. A circle with a lot of lines through it. I didn't know what to make of it."

"Have another look when you get home and you'll see that all the planets are on there. Or don't look. It doesn't really matter. It's what you do with your month that matters."

"You're talking in riddles again, Uri."

"Okay. In simple language. Once a month, every month, somewhere on the planet one girl is chosen to be a Zodiac Girl. What this means is that she gets the help of the ten planets, who are here on Earth in human form. What she does with this help is up to her. It usually happens when the girl is at some kind of turning point in her life."

"Why can't you just say, 'once a month, we at Celestial Weddings pick someone to receive our special promotion? The offer only lasts a month'— you can repeat that part if you want because it seems to be important to you—'There are ten of us in the business, and we will be there to help.' There. That's it. Simple. You don't need to mess it up with talking about astrology and stuff because some people aren't into that and you may lose customers."

Uri's eyes were glistening and I wondered if I'd gone too far and upset him. Then I realized that his face had a strange expression because he was trying not to laugh. Shame, because I liked him even though he was a bit odd, and I had only been trying to help.

"Okay, Chloe," he said after he'd composed his face. "Just go with the flow, Zodiac Girl, and be open to what you can learn. Do what Librans do best and see both sides."

"Hermie said that, too," I muttered, and Uri continued saying something else about being a Zodiac Girl, but I wasn't really listening anymore because Marcie finally came out in her suit. She looked really pretty with her hair pulled up in the back.

"Ready?" she asked.

I nodded.

"Okay, we can do this one of two ways," said Uri. "The wedding suits are made of Velcro, so after the ceremony, when the minister says, 'I now pronounce you husband and wife,' the bride and groom simply hurl themselves at each other and *splat*, they are as one. Joined from head to toe in Holy Matrimony. And Velcro."

Marcie giggled. "Sam will love it."

*Crazy*, I thought, but I didn't say anything because today was just for having fun, not for making serious decisions, and I also knew that there were several options left on Marcie's list after this.

"Come on, Chloe," said Uri. "Let's show your sister how it's done. Let's stand side by side and when I clap, let's jump toward each other." He clapped his hands, we jumped, and our suits welded together. It was hysterical because he was over six feet tall and I am only five foot four, so I was stuck to his side but my feet were dangling. "Joined at the hip," I said as he walked off down the room with me firmly clasped to him.

"Isn't that what they say about some married couples?"

Uri laughed.

"What's the second way of doing it?" asked Marcie.

Uri indicated a ladder that led up onto the trampoline. "For the more adventurous," he said. He climbed up and held out a hand to me. I clambered on after him and smiled at Nessa, who was still up there. Trampolining was something that I could do. Demi had one in her backyard, and we used to go on it every Saturday when we were younger. Nessa winked and gave us the thumbs-up.

"Okay," said Uri. "Imagine that I'm the groom." He began to jump up and down, up and down, and then he hurled himself against the wall, flinging out his arms and legs as he did so. And there he stayed, suspended halfway up the wall. "See, the wall is made of Velcro, too. Come on, Nessa."

Nessa bounced and threw herself toward Uri, and there she was, splatted beside him. "Give it a try, Chloe," she said. "Come on, Marcie—join in."

I jumped and jumped, splayed my arms out, and went for the wall, where I stuck like glue. "Come on, Marcie," I called.

She climbed the ladder and then tentatively began to jump.

"Aim for the wall after your next spring," said Uri. "You don't have to be good at trampolining. It's just there to give you a launching pad onto the Velcro."

Marcie bounced higher, and then she flung herself at the wall. When she realized that she was safe and not going to fall off, she smiled a little. "And how do you get down?" she asked.

"Easy," Uri replied. "I'll show you."

I looked over at Uri and the situation suddenly struck me as really funny. The four of us hanging halfway up a wall, having a conversation like it was totally normal. *Once again, not the typical wedding scenario,* I thought, but I was beginning to see that it could be fun and that I had been too closed to Marcie's suggestions in the beginning. I let out a little giggle.

"Humor. Exactly," said Uri. "See, getting married can sometimes turn into an intense occasion, and the two people who are supposed to be enjoying it the most end up being miserable and stressed. The Velcro experience brings an element of the unexpected into it all. Why go for the boring old convention? Be a rebel on your wedding day, surprise your guests— that's what I say. Live a little, have fun. And in answer to your question, Marcie, to get down you simply peel yourself away, limb by limb." He peeled away his right arm, then his left, his right leg, then his left, then he leaned forward and peeled his spine away from the wall, pushed off with his feet, and leaped back onto the trampoline.

There was no stopping me after that. I bounced with Uri and Nessa. We tried splaying on the wall with our arms and legs in different positions. Marcie had a few tries, but she didn't seem to be enjoying it as much as Uri, Nessa, and me. Uri was amazing at it. He could do a somersault in the air and stick to the wall upside down. "Ta-da!" he said with a grin after one amazing leap.

"Wow! Now that would be impressive. If Sam could do that! Don't you think, Marcie?" I said.

"Maybe," she said. She had a pensive look on her face. "I'll have to think about it. Might be a bit difficult for doing the toast though, or cutting the cake."

"We could find a way," I said. "This gets my vote."

Marcie didn't say anything. We climbed down from the trampoline and I took her aside. "You okay?"

"I'm not sure this is for me," she said, and her bottom lip wobbled a little. "I mean, imagine the wedding photos."

"But Nessa said she can make a pretty outfit," I said.

"In Velcro! You've changed your tune," said Marcie. "What's the matter with you? I thought you wanted the best for me. Silk and lace and tiny mother-of-pearl beads."

"I . . . I . . . Marcie, it's *your* list. I'm trying to be helpful." I decided to quote what Nessa had said. "I am trying to see both sides, be easygoing. Nessa says—"

Marcie wasn't appeased. "Nessa this, Nessa that. You've just met her."

"I know, but honest, Marcie, if you'd seen her gorgeous designs at the wedding show and met her colleagues, you'd be impressed, too. And I won some kind of astrology thing where I get her advice for a month. And she does talk sense."

"You've fallen under her spell because she's so beautiful. And you're not the only one who knows about astrology, you know. I had a roommate when I was in college who was a Libran, and there's another trait I remember about them. Easily influenced. And that's you. Adamant about one thing one week and then someone comes along and turns your head."

"Hey! That's so not fair," I said. "I . . . I . . ."

"Yeah. You hate me. Go on, say it. Be the princess who didn't get her way."

*What on earth is going on?* I asked myself. *Planning a wedding is supposed to be such a happy thing to do, but this is turning weird. I don't seem to be able to do anything right. I resist Marcie's plans and she says I'm selfish. I go along with them and try to get into it and she accuses me of being easily influenced. I can't win!* I decided to shut up and not say another word.

After I'd changed back into my jeans and T-shirt, we said goodbye and thank you to Uri and Nessa and drove home. It was a silent trip, both of us wearing sulky expressions, me with my arms firmly crossed over my chest. I glanced over at Marcie. *It's you who's acting like a spoiled princess, blaming everyone else for Sam's stupid list*, I thought, as I mentally struck option two from the list.

"Sam ought to be here with you doing this," I said. I'm just your sister. It's not my fault you aren't enjoying this."

"Don't I know it," she said through gritted teeth. "Sam is probably sitting in a sports bar somewhere having the time of his life. The way I feel at the moment, I think I'd like to tell him off rather than marry him."

*Oops!* I thought.

# Chapter Eight

# Options Schmoptions

"How is your eighth-grade project going, Chloe? Have you chosen a career path yet?" asked my sister Jane as she forked her way through Mom's casserole, picking out the mushrooms.

*Not this again!* I thought. "I might become a trampoline artist in the circus," I replied. "Or maybe a window cleaner. I can't decide." I thought I was being quite funny, but nobody laughed.

"This is important, Chloe," lectured Clare, my other sister. "The lawyers that I interviewed for my eighth-grade presentation helped me get into law school." I rolled my eyes. I had heard this story a thousand times.

"Marcie was right about you being easily influenced, you know," Clare continued. "Not because you're a Libran—we all know that astrology is a bunch of baloney—but because you just are and always have been."

"Duh! I was joking," I protested. It was the evening

after Marcie and I had been to the Incredible Velcro place, and my sisters had come over for supper. Sadly, what should have been a nice girlie time with us discussing Marcie's wedding and what we were going to wear was fast turning into a character assassination of the worst kind, that character being me. I looked at each of them in turn. Even if you didn't know them, you would know that they were sisters. Like Marcie, Jane and Clare take after my mom and have her chestnut brown hair, brown eyes, fine features, and slightly small mouth. I'm the only blond of the girls in our family and the only one with a dimple, right in the middle of my chin. I take after Dad, who was fair when he had hair (but he was pretty much bald the last time I saw him). I wonder sometimes if they are mean to me because I look like him and they don't want to be reminded.

"Gullible is the word I'd use," said Clare.

"You're always changing your mind, it's true," said Mom.

"That's not a bad thing," I protested. "There are two sides to every story, and surely you, Clare, as a lawyer, ought to know that."

Clare raised her eyebrows and fixed me with a stern look. "Only one side wins though."

"Okay, if I am easily influenced then what about Marcie? Before she met Sam Hunkalunk, she wanted a normal wedding in a beautiful dress with a fabulous reception. Instead, we're on some kind of weird adventure week." As I said the words, though, I remembered what Nessa and Uri had said about not settling for convention and the fun of being a rebel and doing something wacky. Despite my first choice still being the traditional wedding, I wasn't as one hundred percent against Sam's list as I had been in the beginning. The alternatives didn't have to be tacky. With the right organization and Nessa to help, they could possibly be made to work. "I'm trying to be open-minded, and that's more than you three are about astrology. It's actually very scientific."

Jane grinned. "You know, you could make a good lawyer, Chloe. You do know how to argue."

"Pff!" I said.

Clare laughed. "Pff? Yes, very articulate for a wannabe lawyer."

"I'm not a wannabe lawyer," I protested. "I'm a wannabe don't-know-what-I-wannabe." Through all the banter, I noticed that Marcie was quiet, and I wondered if she was still mad at me for enthusing about the Velcro idea and the roller skating. "You okay, Marcie?"

She gave an unconvincing nod.

"She's having wedding nerves, aren't you, dear?" asked Mom.

Marcie shrugged. "Not sure what I'm having. Not sure I'll even be having a wedding. I mean, maybe we should just skip that part and do what you did, Jane, with Michael—just live together. Maybe Sam was right—who needs a wedding in this day and age?"

I could not believe my ears! *First she shatters my dreams by saying she doesn't want a conventional wedding, and I've been doing my best to get over that and be easygoing. I've tried to compromise and go along with the plan and now she's thinking about giving up on that, too.* I looked over at my sisters and wondered if I might be adopted. I watched them sitting there with their neat features to match their neat clothes. Jane and Clare like to wear navy a lot—perfectly tailored suits and polished shoes to go with their polished lives. I like pink and pretty pastel colors and makeup and dressing up. Jane and Clare used to share a room when they lived here, and even that was always neat. It was painted a soft gray and packed with books—not fun books but books about facts. I used to share a room with Marcie, but as soon as Jane and Clare moved out, I got their old room and the first thing I did was paint it baby pink and put up my wedding posters. My sisters were *horrified*. I used to think Marcie and I were a bit alike, but the older she gets, the more like the others she becomes. So yes, adopted. Maybe. No, not maybe. I must be. Definitely. *I wish someone like Nessa was my real mother,* I thought.

*Someone with a sense of style who likes beautiful things in life and seems to get me.*

"I despair. I am going up to my room, and I don't want to talk to anyone, okay?" I said.

Clare shrugged, Jane continued picking out her mushrooms, Marcie stared out the window with a moody expression on her face, and Mom just smiled. "Don't forget to think about your project," she said as though she hadn't even noticed that my sisters were picking on me.

I went up and sat on the window ledge and stared out into the dark. *I don't know where I fit in this life,* I thought. *On the one hand, I know exactly who I am: Chloe Bradbury. I live at 23 Midhurst Street; I know I am the youngest of four girls and I go to school. On the other hand, I have no idea who I am or what I should do. But it didn't seem to matter until now. Why can't I just be me? A schoolgirl? That's my career for now.* I spent another few minutes thinking about career topics for my project. *Fashion maybe. I like clothes and design. Or maybe travel? I am good at languages. I could do tours or translating. But maybe I'd miss home. Maybe I should stay here and . . . open a store. I have a good eye. I could make it look beautiful.* I wrote down my various options and then sighed. Mom and my sisters were right—I did keep changing my mind. I needed something to cheer myself up, so I got down from the ledge and pulled out the tote bag with all my wedding stuff in it. Looking through the glossy pages usually gave me a lift, but this time, as I flipped through the pages and stared at the beautiful dresses and the wonderful locations, none of the gloss rubbed off on me. My sure-fire method to make myself feel better was failing me, and I felt flat. Maybe happy wedding days only happened to other people, not to me or Marcie or anyone else in the Bradbury family.

# Chapter Nine

# The Madness Continues

*Call Nessa,* said a voice in my head as I waited in our front room for Demi, Maryam, and Marcie to arrive. I had been reading over my horoscope and thinking about what it all meant. *She said she's here to help. Special offer, one month only.* I pressed the button next to her name, and she picked up immediately.

"Hello, darlin'."

"Nessa, heeeelp! I have been trying your way of doing things and it doesn't seem to be working out, and now Marcie is angrier than ever with me. What should I do?"

"Hang tough, doll. You have to give it a bit longer," she said. "I know you might be losin' patience, but that's because you have Aries risin'—"

"Aries rising? I thought I was a Libran. What do you mean, I have Aries rising?"

"Sun signs change every month accordin' to the date that a person is born, so everyone born on September twenty-third to October twenty-second is born under the Sun sign of Libra," Nessa explained. "But have you ever wondered why all Librans are not the same? You'll have some similar traits, but you'll all be individuals, and that's because there are other planets and factors besides your Sun sign that affect your horoscope, and one of them is your risin' sign."

"So what's that then? Isn't that Libra, too?"

"No. Sun signs change every month, but a risin' sign changes every two hours, which is why different people born on the same day will be different— because although, say, they are all born on September twenty-eighth, they won't all be born at four o'clock in the mornin'. Some will be born at six, others at eight and so on, and so they will all have different risin' signs."

"Oh. I remember Uri saying something like that. I've been reading over my chart and trying to understand that, too. It's pretty complicated, isn't it?"

"Don't worry, Chloe, it takes a while to sink in. You were born at six o'clock in the evenin', and the risin' sign at that time on that date was Aries. At eight o'clock it changed to Taurus, and at ten o'clock it changed to Gemini, and so on, through all the signs."

"And that makes everyone individual unless, of course, you are born at the same time, at the same hour, and in the same place as someone else."

"Exactly. You're a bright kid. Your Sun sign

determines your general characteristics—how you look, how you are on a superficial level—but your risin' sign also contributes to your personality, and you have Aries risin', which will sometimes make you impetuous and impatient. People who have a strong Aries in their charts tend to be leaders and have lots of energy, but they also tend to rush at things."

"I think I understand," I said.

"Just be patient, go through the list with Marcie, put all the cards on the table before you say what you think should or shouldn't happen."

"You're saying that I have to slow down. I think I can do that," I said. "Already the first two options on the list didn't turn out how I thought they would." Nessa put things so nicely that it all seemed do-able, and I felt okay—unlike when my family spoke to me, when it always seemed that I was doing something wrong. "So will I see you today, Nessa?"

"Not me, but you'll see Uri."

"Great," I said. I liked Uri. "Got to go—I can see Marcie's car pulling up."

"Have a good day, then. Laters, Zodiac Girl."

"Laters, Nessa." Talking to her had made me feel a million times better, and I went to open the door for Marcie feeling optimistic about trying out another option on the list.

\* \* \*

"What's up with Marcie?" whispered Demi as we squeezed into the back of Marcie's car with Maryam.

I shrugged. "Marcie, what's up?"

"Nothing. I'm fine," she said unconvincingly.

Maryam grimaced at me, and Demi and I nodded. Fine she definitely wasn't. I decided to try to cheer her up by being mega-cooperative.

"Hey, it's bungee jumping today, isn't it, Marcie? Should be fun."

"Maybe," she replied in a gloomy tone, "but I might skip it. We'll see."

*Amazing,* I thought. *Nessa was so right about everything. I am hardly having to object at all because Marcie seems to be talking herself out of all the options on her own without my having to make a scene.*

"We should at least see what's involved," I said. It was a lesson for life, I decided—go with the flow, keep an open mind, and watch how everything changes, including how people feel about things.

The Bungee Bride branch of Celestial Weddings was located on the ground floor of a tall office building on the outskirts of Osbury.

Uri emerged from the back room as we came in the front door.

"You again," I said with a smile.

"Yes," he replied. "I told you I did the wackiest weddings." He gave me a wink. "Good to see you again, and glad you're up to try another alternative. Impressive."

"Nah," mumbled Marcie, who still didn't look happy at all.

Uri handed us a brochure that showed all the things you could bungee jump off of.

"Can you think of a better way to seal the deal than by jumping off the nearest bridge or tall building, arms entwined with your loved one?" he asked.

I looked up from the "interesting" structures from which you could throw yourself into oblivion. "Duh, yeah!" I said. "But I am trying to remain open-minded until we have been through the whole list."

Demi's face was white. "Please, *please*, Marcie. Please don't make us do this. I didn't realize when I agreed to come that it was bungee jumping today, and I want to be a good friend, but I hate heights. I'll be sick."

*And get whiplash*, I thought. But I decided that now would be the time to share my "path of least resistance" attitude toward life.

"Chill," I said. "It'll be fun!"

"I won't make *you* do it," said Marcie. "All you and Chloe and Maryam have to do is be bridesmaids and look pretty."

I gave Demi a smug look. I was right. It would be fine.

"It's Sam and I who have to make the jump," she added.

I wanted to ask Marcie if she'd gone completely insane, but I was beginning to think that maybe she had. Maybe this was what love did to you. Turned you into a total nut job. I handed her the brochure.

She took it and perused the options. "Okay. A challenge. We don't have to decide anything yet, do we?"

Uri shook his head. "No. We have plenty of time to work out the details. Now follow me, girls, and I'll show you how it's done."

He led us out of his office into the hallway, where we took an elevator up to the twentieth floor. On the roof of the building, it was cold and breezy, and we all pulled our coats tighter around us to keep out the wind. On the corner of the flat roof was a crane that went up and up into the sky. Marcie looked at it and gulped. I took her hand. *She ought to be backing out about now,* I thought, but she took a step toward the crane.

"You don't have to do this," I said.

"I do," she said in an unhappy voice. "Sam called last night to see how it was going. He's so sorry he can't be here and said I have to be his ears and eyes in this. He calls every night and loves hearing about what we're doing. I can't back out now."

Uri ushered us onto a platform with low walls. *Duh? Path of least resistance? This isn't supposed to be happening,* I thought. Uri closed the gate, pressed the control buttons, and we were swung up and into the sky.

"Warghhhhh!" Marcie, Maryam, Demi, and I screeched as one. We reached for each other's hands and clung on to for dear life.

"It's perfectly safe," Uri promised, and he swung us up even higher. I dared a peek. The ground below appeared farther and farther away. "Arggghhh!"

"This is the typical height that people jump from," said Uri. "Look, Chloe, you can see for miles in every direction. Look around, breathe it in."

I had my eyes shut tight. "No. No way. Marcie, this is crazy. Sam should be doing this. It's not fair that he's not here to see for himself how scary it is. I don't care about not resisting. I hate this. It's insane. Please. Enough. Marcie. Uri. Please let's go back now."

I opened my eyes to look at them pleadingly. Marcie took a peep over the edge. "Um . . . yes," she said as she stepped back from the edge. "C-can we go down now, Uri?"

"You're the boss," he said. "It's your wedding."

"No she isn't," I said. "Sam's the boss. It's *his* wedding." I couldn't help it. It was out before I could bite my tongue. I felt the platform lurch and my stomach clenched with fear. I so hoped that it was safe.

Moments later, the movement stopped. "You can open your eyes now, girls," said Uri. "We're back on the roof."

We opened our eyes and I took a deep breath of relief.

"Well, that gives you some idea how it might feel. Exhilarating, huh?" said Uri. "And you can choose the location. We can do it from most tall buildings or a bridge or a canyon, whatever you prefer."

"I think I'd prefer a cup of tea on level ground," said Marcie. Maryam and Demi and I nodded back at her.

"There's also our parachute-dive wedding. It's going to be very popular. Would madam like to see a video?" Uri called after us after he'd opened the gate and we headed for the door that led to the elevator. "Or maybe you'd like to hear about our paragliding wedding? That's a super option. You can do it together while your guests watch from the cliff edge. It's beautifully symbolic—a couple stepping over the edge, sailing into the unknown." For a moment, Uri looked dreamy, and I wondered if he'd ever been in love.

In the meantime, Demi looked like she was going to throw up.

"That was truly *horrible*," she groaned, "and we didn't even jump. Remind me again why we're doing this."

"For Sam," said Marcie in a clipped voice. "He wants the day to be fun."

"Fun, yes. Terrifying, no. Isn't the fact that you're marrying him enough?" I asked. "Won't *that* make the day fun?"

Marcie shrugged. "It should, shouldn't it? I don't know. I want to make him happy. And marriage is a partnership. I have to give his suggestions a chance."

"You want to make him happy, but what about you, Marcie? I can honestly say I've never seen you more *un*happy than this week," I said, and Demi and Maryam nodded in agreement. I knew that I was going against everything that Nessa had advised, but she hadn't been up there, miles above the ground.

A flash of irritation crossed Marcie's face. "Well, nothing is decided," she said in a clipped tone, "and we still have a few more options to try." But I noticed that her hand was shaking as she crossed option three off the list.

We went back to our house later that day, and while Marcie was out with Mom, Demi, Maryam, and I paged through our bridesmaids' album in great sadness, as though someone in it had died.

"We have to face it," I said. "We have to let go of what we want. It has to be *her* dream wedding, not ours."

"Yes," said Demi and Maryam listlessly.

I picked up my zodiac phone, which was beeping that I had a message. **Let's not be rigid in our thinking**, it said. It was from Dr. Cronus, AKA Saturn. I read it out loud to the girls.

"Whatever," said Demi.

"I guess," said Maryam. "We haven't met Dr. Cronus, have we?"

I shook my head. "No, and I don't think he was at the wedding show either."

The zodiac phone beeped again. This time it said, **Life is determined not by what happens but by how you respond to what happens,** from Dr. Cronus again. I read it out loud in a snooty voice, and Demi and Maryam cracked up.

"Well, I would have thrown up if we'd stayed up on that crane," said Maryam. "That's how I would have responded."

"Me, too," said Demi.

"But we're agreed," I said. "We'll go along with the list with no objections until she decides?"

"And then can we object?" asked Demi.

"Um, not really," I said. "Her wedding, not ours."

"We'll put our own desires aside for Marcie's happiness," said Demi, sighing dramatically.

"Even if it means madness," said Maryam.

"I suppose," I said in a hushed voice. "That will be my motto from now on: Her wedding, not mine."

As we sat looking through my album, I realized that I had to stop agonizing about how it could have been if we had done it my way. Poor Marcie. It *was* her wedding, and I had been insensitive by not really listening to what she wanted. *I know she's trying to please Sam*, I thought, *and maybe that's enough, but . . . I wonder what she really wants in her heart.*

# Chapter Ten

# Underwater Bride

Thursday was number four on the list—the underwater wedding. Marcie, Maryam, Demi, and I were sitting snug as bugs in the Europa deli in Osbury, sipping mugs of hot chocolate made by Joe Joeve, the owner, before we went to the aquarium. It was raining so hard outside that we could have had an underwater wedding in the street, so we weren't in any hurry to get going.

Marcie had a brochure on the table in front of her. "Sam, the minister, and I swim in a giant fish tank," she explained. "You girls wear wet suits, flippers, and goggles with pieces of seaweed woven though your hair. The rest of the guests watch from outside the tank. For music, we could have the sound of whales or dolphins honking in the distance."

"And no doubt you would serve seafood at the reception?" Demi asked innocently.

Marcie nodded. "Yes. I think that's the idea."

"Maybe you and Sam could jump out of the tank when it's time for wedding cake—you know, like feeding time for the dolphins at Sea World," said Maryam, equally innocently.

"Ohmi*cod*!" said Demi. "At least the photos will be different. No one will have wedding pics to top us in scuba gear."

I knew that they were joking at Marcie's expense, but I couldn't blame them. All her wedding guests would laugh, too, if she didn't come to her senses soon. In the meantime, though, I had sworn to myself that I would be supportive to the very last option on the list. "I'm sure Nessa could make you something gorgeous, Marcie. A little swimsuit in white with some lovely freshwater pearls sewn onto it. It might actually look really cool, the two of you swimming, your hair flowing out behind you."

"You seem to have forgotten that I can't put my head under the water, never mind *swim* under water," sighed Marcie. "It seems to have slipped Sam's mind, too, although he would probably say anything is possible if you have the right attitude and then arrange for me to have diving lessons before the wedding."

I had forgotten. Marcie can swim but she's never liked it. Some stupid boy dunked her head under when she was in elementary school, and now she gets panicky in the water. Maybe Sam didn't know how much it freaked her out, but then maybe she hadn't told him. It seemed that she wanted to please him so much that she didn't always tell him what she was feeling about things.

"So are we going to go along for a demo or not?" I asked. I wondered if Nessa would show up with one of her planet colleagues. I had noticed on my zodiac phone that one of them was named Captain John Dory—AKA Neptune. Neptune was the king of the sea, so out of all of Nessa's colleagues, he was the one I'd expected to see today.

"Demo?" asked Marcie. "*Demo?* I'll give that Sam Hendy a demo he won't forget in a hurry." The sharpness in her voice took me by surprise. She very deliberately got a pen out of her bag, and with a dramatic flourish, she crossed out number four on the list. "There. That's what I think of your aquarium wedding, Sam Hendy. You can take your wedding list and shove it—"

An elderly lady at the next table glanced up.

"Marcie," I warned before she said anything embarrassing. "We're in public." Part of me was glad that Marcie was at last seeing sense, but I hate it when people make a scene.

Marcie noticed the woman and rolled her eyes. "Sorry. I'm engaged to the world's greatest IDIOT and I've only just realized it!"

"Lucky you," said the lady. "Better to realize it now than in twenty years when it's too late."

"Exactly!" said Marcie. "Now then, who's up for a big piece of that chocolate fudge cake I saw at the counter before? It's about time we girls had some real fun!"

*Now what's happening?* I wondered as she got up and ordered four huge pieces of cake. As she stood at the counter, my zodiac phone beeped that I had a message from Nessa. **An encounter with Pluto means transformation,** it said. I was about to text back and ask what she meant when Marcie reappeared with our fudge cake.

"When the going gets tough, the tough eat chocolate cake," she said.

"Good plan," said Demi.

"Best one yet," said Maryam, and as we all dug in, I thought that the main transformation was going to be on our waistlines.

"Sam can't accuse me of not trying," said Marcie when later the same day she parked outside Jungle Jamboree, a shop that had gorilla costumes in the window. After we ate our cake and the rain had finally stopped, Marcie had insisted that we try out the last option on the list.

"She is joking, isn't she?" whispered Demi as we got out and followed her into the store.

"I think so," I said. "I'm not sure." I looked at

Marcie. Something had happened this morning, and she had a determined expression on her face—like she'd made up her mind about something and there was no going back.

"Option number five, the Bridezilla wedding," Marcie announced once we got inside to find an empty store. She dinged a bell on the counter to alert whoever owned the place that they had customers. "The idea is that Sam and I wear gorilla outfits. You girls would be chimps."

"Are you serious?" asked Demi.

"I'm not but Sam was, and how *ridiculous* is that?" said Marcie. "But as long as we're here, we may as well explore all the costume options so that when I report back, he knows that I did the job thoroughly and he can't blame me for . . . well, for what I've decided." There was something in her tone that made me think that Sam was in for a telling off. A big telling off.

A few moments later, an extraordinary looking man came from behind a curtain at the back. He was tall and pale and looked every inch a goth prince—he was dressed in a purple velvet suit, and his dark hair was tied back in a ponytail. He gave us a small bow.

"Hello, ladies, and vat are ve looking for today?" he asked in an accent that I couldn't quite place—maybe Russian?

"Great Dracula costume," Demi said.

The man looked affronted. "Dracula? But dis is not da costume. Dis is 'ow I am normally dressing."

Demi grinned. "And you have a great accent, too."

The man bowed again. "P. J.'s da name, transformation da game." He indicated the rows and rows of costumes.

"Ah. You're Pluto, aren't you?" I asked. "Nessa said we might see you."

"And you must be da Zodiac Girl, *Ja*?"

I smiled. "Chloe's da name—"

"Being bonkers da game," Demi joined in.

"Do you know this man?" asked Marcie.

I shook my head. "No, but he's in the wedding business with Nessa, right?"

"I am in da business of change, transformation, like da caterpillar to da butterfly and yes, for dis month, ve is doing the vedding. Other times I do interior design or makeovers."

"Fab," said Demi.

"We're here to look at the gorilla costumes," said Marcie. "For my wedding."

P. J. smiled. "Now dat I can help vith," he said and pointed us in the direction of a rack of furry costumes. "Da Bridezilla vedding is very popular. 'Elp yourselves to anyzing else you vould like to be trying," he said. "I 'ave some jobs to do vhile you are dressing."

He fluttered his hands at us as if to say that we should get on with the business of dressing up.

Dutifully, we looked through the rack, found our sizes, and then went to put our monkey costumes on.

Demi and I were ready first. We looked at each other and burst out laughing. We stood in front of a full-length mirror while we waited for Marcie. We looked totally silly.

"Not exactly what I had in mind for my first bridesmaid outfit," I said as I did a twirl.

"I know it's not," said Demi, her voice muffled by the chimp's head. "You're taking this very well, Chloe. For someone who wanted to dress in silk and lace."

"It's not over yet," I said. "If I thought this madness was going to happen for real, I think I would be freaked out of my mind, but Nessa has been so great telling me to chill and see what happens, and you know what? It has been a fun week."

"And it looks like you won't have to do a crazy wedding in the end," said Demi. "After this morning, I think Marcie has finally seen the light."

"Maybe," I said. "Nessa was so right. She said that if I didn't resist it would be okay. And now Marcie has come to the conclusion by herself that this isn't her dream wedding. It's weird, isn't it? Like we've both changed our minds. She thinks the list is stupid now, and I actually think some of the options have potential."

We high-fived each other just as Maryam came out of the changing room. She made a noise like a chimp and immediately Demi and I joined in and started aping around doing funny monkey walks and noises and having a great time, although it was hard to breathe with the costume heads on. P. J. didn't seem to mind us messing around. He looked over at us and gave us the thumbs-up. Inside, I felt a huge sense of relief about Marcie's turnaround. The Bridezilla option was the one I had worried about the most. It wasn't dangerous or scary, just funny and different, and it might have appealed to Marcie's sense of mischievousness and her love of a practical joke. There had been a distinct possibility that she might go for it before her change in mood today.

"At least we won't have to worry about having our hair done," said Demi as she pretended to try to climb up the dressing room curtains.

"Okay, I'm ready, girls," said Marcie from behind the curtain.

I began to sing the wedding march. "Dah dah da daahh, dah dah da—" I whipped back the curtain of the dressing room, and there, moving very slowly as if walking down an aisle, was a large gorilla. A gorilla wearing a white veil and a tiny tiara and carrying a bunch of white roses. We burst out laughing, and then Marcie began to goof off with us as if we really were a family of chimps. Demi started to groom me, then I pretended to pick bugs from her fur and eat them, and it wasn't long before we were on the floor laughing.

Demi made us line up so she could take a group photo with her phone.

"So, what do you think, Marcie?" I asked after Demi had taken her shot.

"Bit hot," she replied, and she pulled the gorilla head off. "People must be insane to consider this as a wedding option. I mean, aside from the fact that we all look totally stupid, it's roasting in these costumes."

Maryam, Demi, and I took our costume heads off, too. "Whew!" said Maryam. "Yeah. It is kind of hard to breathe in there." We all looked flushed from wearing so much fur.

"There are endless possibilities," said Marcie as she looked around the store, "not just gorillas."

"Go right ahead," said P. J. "Try everything. Be transforming yourselves!"

"Thanks," we chorused. *FABulous,* I thought. I loved dressing up, and there were tons of great-looking costumes.

Marcie picked through a rack at the front of the store. "We could all dress as Superheroes. How about Spiderman?" she asked as she held up a Spiderman outfit. "Sam could swing in from the building across the street from the church. Or we could dress as

Batman and Robin. That should make it special."

I took a long look at her to try and gauge if she was serious. She was still flushed from wearing the big gorilla head, but there was something in her tone that worried me. I wasn't sure if she was sad about Sam or mad at him.

"Or we could do Victorian or goth or vampires or cavemen," she continued, holding up a plastic a club. "I could bash Sam over the head after I've taken the vows."

*Hmm, maybe mad at him,* I thought as she swished the club through the air with some force.

I could have agreed with Marcie about how stupid the costume option was, but I was determined not to crack now, having gotten so far. It looked as if Marcie was figuring it all out on her own. I picked up a horned helmet. "Or what about Vikings?" I asked.

"Yeah, perfect," said Marcie. "Or Robin Hood and Maid Marion? Or *Star Trek* characters?"

"Are you two on drugs?" asked Demi. "What is going on?"

Another costume caught Marcie's eye, and she rushed over, picked out a long white dress, and held it up against her. "A Princess Leia outfit. We could have a *Star Wars* wedding." She looked at her reflection holding up the white dress. It was as close to a normal wedding outfit as there was in the store.

"Ve have da vedding dresses," said P. J. "You is coming up da stairs. All by Nessa. She is up dere making, creating, sewing da dresses."

We all looked at each other.

"Wouldn't do any harm to just try," I said.

"Just a little look," said Demi.

"It is best to consider all options," said Maryam.

"Nessa also does da 'air and makeups," said P. J.

Up we went without any more persuasion. It was like walking into a fairy grotto, with silver, white, and mirrored walls, little lights strewn everywhere like at Christmas, and it smelled divine. Rows of beautiful white and cream dresses hung on rails along the walls, with a couple of examples on dummies toward the back of the room. On a counter to the left were tiaras in mother-of-pearl and diamonds, one of white leaves and another made from what looked like silver leaves. On the wall to the right were shelves of fabric: silk, satin, velvet. It was wedding heaven. We oohed and aahed. I felt like I had found my true home.

"Nessa, ve 'ave customers," said P. J.

We heard a rustle, and a moment later Nessa appeared. She was wearing one of her creations, a sheath in gossamer silk that fell from her shoulders to her feet. Her hair was up and she had on a tiny crown. She was one hundred percent goddess.

"What do you think?" she asked. "This is a new dress that I've been working on."

"Divine," we chorused.

"Thanks," she said. "Now then. How can we help? First of all though, P. J., let's have some bubbly for the bride to be. And are you hungry? Bring some chocolate for the girls, please." She glanced over and winked. "I do think that planning a wedding needs to be fun on every level, don't you? Let's put on some music, too."

P. J. scurried downstairs while Nessa put on some upbeat music. The next hour went by in a happy blur as each of us tried on the prettiest dresses and gulped sparkling cider while Marcie drank champagne with peach juice. We ate scrumptious chocolates with fudge centers and boogied around to the music. Marcie tried on tons of different outfits and every shoe that Nessa showed her, from stunning high-heeled silver sandals to little ballet shoes made from the softest leather. Everything looked good, but Nessa wasn't satisfied. She insisted that Marcie try on the new dress that she'd been wearing. She and P. J. took Marcie away and left Demi, Maryam, and me to continue trying on accessories and flipping through bridal magazines.

"This is what it's all about, isn't it?" I said as I popped another chocolate into my mouth and sat back in one of the plush chairs near the counter. "Great fabrics, heavenly smells, good music. It's a whole experience of loveliness."

Demi did a spin. "Loveliness," she repeated.

Maryam got up to join her but then stopped and stared. "Oh my God!" she said.

Demi and I looked in the direction she was staring. "Oh my God!" we echoed.

Marcie was standing in the doorway wearing the perfect dress. Nessa had done her makeup just perfectly—not too much, just enough to give her face color and a soft glow. Her hair was swept up in a loose knot, and Nessa had threaded pearl beads through the curls. Around her neck she wore a stunning freshwater pearl choker. My eyes filled with tears. Here was my sister Marcie, the bride. This was how she was meant to look. "Oh, Marcie," I said. "You look *beautiful.*"

Marcie stepped forward and looked at herself in the mirror. She caught her breath and her eyes glistened. "I do, don't I?" she whispered.

Behind her, Nessa and P. J. appeared. "Every inch the beautiful bride," said Nessa, then she turned and ushered P. J. away. "Let's leave them alone to talk about it," she said.

As soon as they'd gone, Marcie's eyes filled with the tears she'd been holding back. I went over and put my arm around her shoulder. "You all right?" I asked.

She nodded, but she didn't looked all right.

"You look so beautiful, Marcie," said Demi.

She looked at her reflection and nodded.

"Is this what you really want, Marcie? Is this the sort of wedding outfit you would really like?" I asked.

She sniffed back a tear and nodded. "I'd like to look beautiful on my wedding day. Not in Velcro or on roller skates or under water. I just want to look like a bride."

"Princess for a day," I said.

Marcie nodded. "You guys are the best, you know. You've been so nice this week, going along with everything without complaining, and you, Chloe . . ." she began to sob, "you even tried to roller-skate for me."

"It's your wedding, Marcie," I said. "You should have what *you* want. You were right. I was being selfish in the beginning, trying to make you have *my* perfect wedding when, of course, it's *your* day." I really meant it, too.

I put my arms around her, and she sobbed harder and sniffled into my neck. I let her cry for a while. "Can I do anything? What is it? What's made you so upset?"

Marcie sighed. "You. You have, Chloe. The way you've been this week is amazing, and it's shown me that's what love is, true love. It's giving up what you want to make someone else happy, the way you've done. I know, I know you've had your dream of your day when you get to be a bridesmaid ever since you were little, and I know how much it's meant to you, but you let it all go for me. For me, your big stupid sister with my crazy ideas."

"It's your wedding," I repeated.

Marcie lowered her head. "Yes. It is. And Sam's— more Sam's wedding. I . . . I've been so busy trying to please him and accommodate what he wants that I didn't even tell him what I want and . . . he didn't ask. Hasn't asked! You were right yesterday. Sam should be here with me. We should have been going through this important time together, and he should have asked me what *my* ideas were. I have to have a say, too."

"I'm sure he was going to get around to asking you, and he'll be here for the wedding," I said. "That's the *most* important time when it comes down to it."

Marcie shook her head again. "No. No. I need him now. Or at least I did."

"What do you mean, you did?" I asked. "Have you decided to go ahead with a traditional wedding after all?"

"No," said Marcie. "I have changed my mind about the list and about the wedding. I know going back and forth is usually your thing, Chloe, but this time, it's me. There isn't going to be a wedding, not anymore. I'm through with this whole charade. I'll tell Sam tonight. I have decided, the wedding's off."

# Chapter Eleven

# Doghouse

"What on earth have you done?" asked Clare when she came over that night. Jane had arrived more than an hour earlier and was in the kitchen with Mom, who was trying to comfort Marcie with cups of tea.

"Me? *Nothing*," I replied. Mom had asked the same question just after we'd arrived home and she'd seen Marcie's red eyes. And Jane was barely though the door before she started accusing me. It so wasn't fair.

"You must have said something," Clare insisted. Mom said that Jane said that Marcie said that you said something."

"Me? No. Honest. I asked her what *she* wanted for her wedding, that's all, and . . . and I might have asked where Sam had been while we'd been doing this wedding research, like it seemed to me that he should have been the one trying out all the wacky ideas with her."

Clare clucked her tongue with disapproval. "That will be it, then."

"It's not fair to blame me, Clare. I've done everything

123

I could to support Marcie, even though from the beginning I thought that her wedding ideas were high on the crazy scale. I didn't see you or Mom or Jane exactly volunteering to go bungee jumping or trampolining or dressing up as a gorilla and making fools of yourselves."

"I had to work, but I doubt I'd have done it anyway. In fact, I knew it would all go wrong," said Clare, "as soon as I saw that ridiculous list."

"So you thought it was dumb, too?"

"Yes, of course, but I never actually thought she was going to take it seriously. I credited her with more of a brain. So the wedding's off, I take it?"

"I think so."

"Has she told Sam?"

"She called him not long after we left the costume shop."

"How did he take it?"

"Badly, I think."

"Where is she?"

I jerked my thumb toward the kitchen, and off she went. I couldn't decide what to do or where to go. My head was spinning with choices.

Go into the kitchen with the others? But if Mom wouldn't be blaming me, Clare would be going on about what a letdown men were or Marcie would be crying, so the kitchen wasn't a great option.

Stay put? I could stay in the hall and call Demi or Maryam, who had gone home for supper. Maybe not. What could they say? Or maybe I should—they're my friends after all and understand the situation better than anyone. But then, maybe they'd had enough of all the Bradbury drama.

Bedroom? Should I go upstairs for a cuddle with Sergeant Ted? He was a teddy bear—what could he do? But cuddling him always made me feel better.

Bathroom? Have a long relaxing bubble bath?

Or should I go back in and see Marcie? Maybe I should run a bath for her?

I took a step toward the kitchen. No, that didn't feel right.

I took a step toward the stairs. No, I'd feel out of things up there.

Bathroom? No, it would be wrong to lock myself away at a time like this.

Decisions, decisions. *WHY CAN'T I EVER MAKE UP MY MIND? Things can't possibly get any worse*, I thought, when the phone rang. As there was no movement coming from the kitchen, I picked up. It was Sam.

"Oh!" I gulped. "Hi. Um . . . Sam. I, er . . . do you want to talk to Marcie?"

"No, Chloe, I wanted to talk to you." He sounded sad.

"Oh, well, here I am, yes, it's me," I said, trying to

sound bright and cheerful although that was the last thing I was feeling. "And how are you?"

"How do you think I am, Chloe? How do you *think* I am?"

*Not happy, that's for sure,* I thought. *I can tell that much from your voice.* "Er . . . uh . . . Are you sure you don't want to talk to Marcie? She is here, in the kitchen."

"Marcie has made it very clear that she doesn't want to speak to me. Not now. Not ever again. Says I don't know the true meaning of love. Says you do. Do you, Chloe? Because if you do, maybe you could let me know what it is because it's clearly a mystery to me."

"Me? I don't know anything."

"What should I do? I do love her, you know. More than anything. She is The One and she always has been, but now she hates me for not understanding what she wanted. But how was I supposed to know? How is any guy supposed to know what women want? And now I've lost her."

"Maybe not—" I started.

"I have. And she said it's thanks to you."

"Thanks to me? No, Sam. All I have tried to do is go along with the plan."

"But you never really liked me, did you? Did you say something to turn her against me?"

"I . . . Um. No. Not really." But too late—he'd heard the hesitation in my voice. "Okay. I might have

126

said something about you not listening to what she wanted," I confessed.

"But she never said. I thought she was okay with the list."

"I think she wanted to make you happy. Listen. Let me try to persuade her to talk to you. Hold on."

I put the phone down and raced along the hall to the kitchen, where Marcie was.

"Sam's on the phone," I said urgently. "Will you talk to him? He sounds totally sorry."

Marcie shook her head. "Too late," she said.

I went back to the phone. "Sam, you there? She won't come—"

I was about to say that I would keep trying, but he'd hung up.

I put down the phone and burst into tears. *Now everyone is unhappy*, I thought. *I hate weddings.* Suddenly I knew exactly where I wanted to go. I wanted to go upstairs to my bed, get under the duvet with Sergeant Ted, and never come out again.

# Chapter Twelve

# Meeting the Planets

"So what are you going to do?" asked Demi when I met up with her and Maryam at lunch break on Monday.

"I've decided I'm going to go to Osbury after school. I'm going to find Nessa and give her back the zodiac phone and tell her that I don't want to be a Zodiac Girl or have anything to do with it anymore."

"But why?" asked Maryam. "It's not her fault."

"Yes it is. Sam thinks it's my fault that Marcie called the wedding off, that I talked her out of it, but I didn't, not really. Okay, I may have said a few things, but I never thought this would happen. The last couple of weeks have been the weirdest of my life, and ever since I won that stupid Zodiac thing and Nessa started giving me advice, everything has gone wrong. All that stuff about not resisting and going with the flow. Maybe if I give the prize back, that will fix it. I'll tell them to let some other girl be the Zodiac Girl."

"I'll volunteer for it! If I didn't have to babysit my

brother tonight, I'd come with you and tell them myself," said Maryam. "I'd love to be a Zodiac Girl and have someone like Nessa give me advice."

"And me," said Demi. "If I didn't have my photography class after school, I'd say I'd be the Zodiac Girl. I always thought it looked fun, and there are two weeks left. Who knows what could happen? And Uri said that there could only be one girl chosen at a time. One girl, one month. Remember? So, yeah, maybe if you back out, one of us can take your place— I bet there are lots more wedding goodies to try out."

Hearing Demi and Maryam enthuse about being a Zodiac Girl threw me and made me wonder if I'd made the wrong decision. Maybe it wasn't Nessa's fault. *Oh no*, I thought, *here I go again! Can't make a decision and stick to it.*

"Well, for me it's been a curse, not a blessing," I said as the bell rang and we gathered up our things for our afternoon classes. *Or has it been a blessing?* I asked myself as we made our way to the science lab. *Yes, being blamed for breaking up Marcie's engagement was bad, but trying out the list of wedding options had been fun. It had. Should I give Nessa another chance? See what else she has in store? Arghhh! another decision.* "I think I am going mad," I said.

"*Going* mad? You always were," teased Demi.

"No, really. I *hate* being a Libran. It's supposed to be

129

a nice sign, easygoing, balanced, but I think it's the *worst* sign of the whole zodiac, like—being able to see both sides, it means that it's hard to make a decision about anything. I'm always so busy weighing options and making sure that what I decide is balanced."

"You can't change your birth sign, though," said Maryam. "It's not like changing your name."

"I know. So that's it then. I am doomed for life, cursed for eternity. I will forever not be able to make up my mind about anything and so will have to suffer the consequences. Great, now I'm depressed as well as crazy."

"So make a few choices," said Maryam. "Defy the traits of your birth sign and make a decision. You know Mr. Mooney isn't going to let you slide on your project much longer.

"Oh that. I'd forgotten all about that over the weekend. What with Marcie blubbing all over the place and everyone blaming me and Sam mad at me and being in the doghouse, I'd totally forgotten about that stupid project."

Demi squeezed my arm. "So now you're crazy, and you're depressed and stressed, too," she said.

I nodded. "And it's only Monday! So, okay, I am going to make a choice, and this is it. I am going to go to Osbury, talk to Nessa, and ask just what this whole Zodiac Girl thing is all about. She said she was my guardian and here to help, so get me out of this mess, Nessa—let's see if you can!"

Demi glanced at Maryam. "I suppose it's a start," she said.

Maryam took my other arm. "And we love you whatever you decide or don't decide. To us, you're just Chloe, our lovely friend who can never make up her mind."

After school I caught the bus as usual, but instead of getting off at my stop to go home, I stayed on the bus until it got to Osbury. I'd texted Nessa during my afternoon break and said I'd like to come and see her, and she texted back that she'd be in the Europa deli and that it was perfect timing for me to meet up with her and the others. *Yeah, right,* I'd thought.

Once off the bus, I made my way through the park where the wedding show had been held and saw Europa in front of me. It looked warm and cozy inside, and I was looking forward to one of Joe's fantastic hot chocolate drinks. Inside, the deli was empty apart from Joe, who was busy behind the counter. He looked up and smiled when he saw me. "Ah, ze Zodiac Girl," he said. "Welcome."

"Quiet night," I replied. "Where is everybody?"

"Here in a moment," he said. "Nessa said you wanted to talk. Until then, sit, sit, and I'll bring you your special."

I did as I was told, and soon he set before me a cup of steaming hot chocolate. "Hmm, delicious," I said after I took the first sip. It really was like nothing I had ever tasted before, with just the perfect balance of chocolate and creaminess. Nessa and Uri arrived shortly after, followed by P. J. and Hermie. They waved and then went to get drinks for themselves. *One, two, three, four, five. Five members of the Celestial Wedding company*, I thought. *I wonder where the other five are.*

Hermie, who was looking as handsome as ever, pushed a couple of tables together and beckoned me over.

"So, Chloe," said Nessa once everyone was settled. "You wanted our advice."

"Yes. I mean no. I mean—"

All five of them burst out laughing.

"Why are you laughing?" I asked.

"It's just such a typical Libra trait—yes, no, can't make up your mind," Nessa replied.

"Tell me about it. It's been a nightmare lately. I feel like I've been losing my mind."

The five nodded solemnly, and I felt like they understood.

"What exactly is the problem?" asked Hermie.

"Oh, just everything," I began, and before I knew it, I was telling the whole story from the very beginning, from when I started the Bridesmaids' Club up to last weekend when Sam called me and sounded as unhappy as Marcie and I started thinking that maybe I had turned her against him. The planet people didn't interrupt or make faces like they were judging me. They just listened. "I guess that's it, really," I said when I had finished.

"Hmm, zis iz a tough one," said Joe.

"You can say that again," I said.

"Hmm, zis iz a—," Joe began.

"What about you, Chloe?" interrupted Nessa. "I see you've had a difficult angle with Mars in your horoscope. Is there somethin' else that you're not tellin' us about, darlin'?"

"Er . . . yes . . . no, um, Mars. That's listed as Mario on the phone, isn't it? Why haven't I met him if he's part of my horoscope?"

"Oh, you will," Nessa replied. "Soon in fact. He deals with goals and ambitions. Do those things ring a bell?"

"Sort of. School project. I need to figure out my goals and ambitions and write a big report, and I can't even begin because I haven't a clue."

The five of them laughed again.

"Why do you keep laughing?" I asked. "It's so *not* funny. In fact, these past weeks have been the hardest of my life. I don't get this whole Zodiac Girl thing."

"Some Zodiac Girls get who we really are," said Hermie.

"And ozzers don't. Dey rationalize vot happens to dem to fitting deir understandings of deir world," said P. J.

"Like Chloe," said Nessa. "Doesn't matter though, does it?"

"Maybe it does," said P. J.

*Arrgh! Make up your minds*, I thought as I tried to make sense of what they were trying to tell me. Whatever one said, a moment later another contradicted it. For a second I wondered if they were making fun of me by mimicking my trouble making up my mind.

"Are you making fun of me?" I asked.

Uri grinned. "Maybe, maybe not."

"There *are* different sides to every situation," added Nessa. "Nothin' wrong with seeing that."

"Unless it messes up your head," said Hermie, jutting his chin in my direction.

"Exactly," I said. "It has *really* messed up mine. I don't know what to think or do anymore, and that's why I needed to see you. I need your help."

"How can we help, doll?" asked Nessa gently.

"I need to get Marcie and Sam back together. Okay, she was freaked out by his weird wedding list, but I think that she genuinely does love him. She's been so miserable since they broke up, and he

134

sounded really upset, too."

"Ah," said Nessa. "True love. Now that's something I do know about."

"Marcie said that *I* had shown her what love is, and in doing that I somehow turned her against Sam because he wasn't there for her," I explained. "I didn't mean to do that."

"Ah," said Joe. "But a break might be good for zem. Absence makes ze heart grow fonder."

"Yes and no—sometimes absence makes the heart grow cold and forget," said Uri.

"So what is love then?" I asked. "How do you know when it's true?"

"You feel beautiful and everythin' feels harmonious," said Nessa.

"No," said P. J. "Eet can also be vith pain, passion, torment, a sweet agony, but you can't escape, like an addiction."

"No. It's when you feel like you are your very best self with someone, and they feel like their very best self with you," said Nessa.

"No," said Uri. "It's when you can be at your worst with someone and they still love you, like first thing in the morning when you haven't even combed your hair or when you're having a lousy day and don't feel like seeing anyone."

"No," said Joe. "It's more simple zan zat. Love is

unconditional. You will do and go anywhere for someone without expectations for yourself. The minute there are selfish expectations, then it's not true love, it's selfish love."

"But people are only human," said Nessa.

"But love is divine," said Hermie. "I think true love is when you and your lover are in true communication, like you know what each other thinks and feels."

"No," said P. J. "It's a journey, a learning process."

*They're making fun again,* I thought, *and talk about confusing!* I watched them put forward different arguments and angles and points of view. It was like watching a ball at a tennis match. One side and then the other, back again, then back again, and everything everybody said seemed to be right. Actually, it was like living inside my head, always seeing one side and then the other. These planet people weren't being any help at all. They were as confused as I was and couldn't agree on anything.

"I don't think you know any more than I do," I said.

Nessa smiled. "Yes and no. We were demonstratin' that it's true, there are always many sides to every situation, and even though it's confusin' sometimes, Chloe, seein' the various angles is what gives you your strength."

"Strength to do what?"

"To meet the unexpected as a challenge and adventure," said Uri.

"But how does that help Sam?"

"Hmm. First Sam has to let Marcie go," said Uri. "If love is true, if you let it go and it keeps coming back, then it is meant to be."

P. J. scoffed. "How idealistic is dat? No. You have to vork at it to make love happen. Tell him he has to tell her how he is feelings, voo her to vin her heart again."

"He shouldn't be too intense though, or desperate," said Nessa "Tell Sam to pursue her with flowers, perfume, chocolates."

"Or maybe she should forget him and move on," said Uri.

This time I laughed. "You guys can't make your mind up about anything! You really are worse than me. All you do is contradict each other. You know what? *I* am going to decide."

They all nodded like children who had just been reprimanded.

"Good," said Nessa. "What are you going to do?"

"Romance," I said. "That's something we Librans know about. I am going to call Sam and tell him that in order to win Marcie back, he needs to romance her. I like your plan, Nessa. A lovely evening. Flowers. Maybe a restaurant with gypsy music. Champagne. Moonlight."

Nessa was watching me with a proud expression. "Exactly," she said.

But then another thought occurred to me. "Or do you think the saying 'Treat them mean to keep them keen' is true? Maybe he shouldn't call her, and then she'll miss him and think about him. Sometimes people want what they can't have."

P. J. nodded. "Dat is true. De lure of de unattainable."

"No," said Nessa. "Maybe that would have worked in the beginnin', but these two are too far down the line for that. They were engaged, for goodness sake. They're way past the time of playin' games. No, Chloe, you tell Sam that if he doesn't want to lose Marcie, he has to swallow his pride, buy the most beautiful bunch of flowers he can find, and keep pursuin' her like he's her slave until she gives in."

"I agree," I said. "He must romance her."

"So what are you waitin' for?" asked Nessa with a smile.

Joe got up and got a piece of paper and six pens. "For ze plan," he said.

"Excellent," I said as I took a pen and wrote the word "Romance" at the top of the paper.

# Chapter Thirteen

# Goals, Schmoals

Tuesday went by. Wednesday. Thursday. I hadn't heard from Marcie, I hadn't heard from Sam, and I hadn't heard from Mario, the Mars person, even though Nessa said that I had an encounter with him coming up. I knew I didn't have much time left to work on my project, and I had been up late every night trying to decide, talking it over with Mom and even with Jane and Clare. They all offered what advice they could, and depending on who I last talked to, my career choice kept changing. Fashion, lawyer, vet, art, science, languages—I still couldn't decide. It felt hopeless. I just couldn't make up my mind.

And then on Friday, at assembly, Mr. Fitzpatrick, our headmaster, announced, "We have a very special guest visiting the school today. Mario Ares, teacher of martial arts, ex-soldier, and expert career advisor. If you're in any doubt what your goals are, this is the man to talk to."

*Ta-da!* I thought. *He's my man.*

I signed up immediately and got an appointment for lunch time. As soon as the bell rang, I hurried to the library, where my session was scheduled to take place. A tall handsome black man stood behind a table.

"Ah, Chloe Bradbury. I was wondering when we might meet." He had the same charisma as the other planet people, larger than life. He smiled, revealing a perfect set of Hollywood white teeth. *Nessa and her pals must have the same dentist because they all have perfect teeth*, I thought as I approached him. I felt a rush of adrenalin, like I was about to meet a famous person.

"So, Zodiac Girl," he said as we sat down at the table, facing each other. "Third week in. How's it going?"

"Okay, I guess. Nessa said I only get to be Zodiac Girl for four weeks."

"One month, one girl," said Mario, repeating the words that Uri had said. "I trust you have been making the most of it."

"Yes . . . um, maybe, but what exactly does it mean?"

"Didn't Nessa or one of the others explain?"

"Sort of. Nessa said that for one month, I got the guidance of her as my guardian, plus the help of the other planets that are prominent in my chart. At first I thought it was just a marketing theme. Like, the planet people I've met all seem to be in the wedding business.

But why would they choose the planet theme? I'm beginning to get the feeling that there's more to it. I mean, you're not part of Celestial Weddings and you know about the zodiac thing, so who exactly are you?"

Mario considered me for a moment like he was weighing up who I was and whether I had a brain or not.

"My connection with weddings is that I work with brides and grooms wanting to tone up and get fit for the big day," he said. "You know, as a personal trainer. I set the goals. I put them through their paces. I get results. I get them looking their very best physically. That's my involvement. But you're right—there's more to it than that."

I thought about all the times Nessa and the others had seemed to know exactly when I needed them, about how weird it was that they just happened to offer all the weddings on Sam's list, and how everything about them felt a bit magical. Maybe I would never completely understand what being a Zodiac Girl was all about, but for the moment I was happy just to let them help me, so I decided not to ask any more questions. "Yes, I thought so."

Mario looked at me again as if he was trying to gauge me, and I looked back at him with the same expression.

"Okay, Miss Zodiac. Career choices. Subject choices

for your project?" he finally asked.

"Haven't a clue. Well, I had ideas, but I keep changing my mind. That's because I am a Libran—see, I don't know much about astrology, but I do know that Librans are represented by the symbol of the scales because they like to weigh and balance all sides of an argument before they make up their mind. I used to think it was a weakness, but now Nessa has helped me to understand that it's actually a strength."

Mario looked amused. "Is that so?"

"Why are you laughing? Why do all of you in the planet business laugh at me?"

"Not laughing *at*," said Mario, "laughing *with*. It's a joy to have astrology explained to me . . . And so articulately."

"Well, I don't know how much you know about it," I said. "I don't assume that everyone knows as much about it as I do now. Uri and Nessa have explained a bit about it since I became Zodiac Girl."

"They are to be commended," said Mario.

"Anyway, with the gift of seeing all sides of an argument," I continued, "I could be a lawyer or a psychologist, but then, on the other hand, Librans have a good sense of beauty and harmony, so I could be an artist or designer or something. I'm still not sure."

"Listen to your gut and then go for it," said Mario. "From all I have heard from Nessa and the others, I would have thought that your perfect job was staring you right in the face."

"My face? My perfect job? No. What?"

"Sometimes people miss what is right in front of them. I can't tell you though. It has to come from you."

"Give me a clue," I said.

"It's a natural talent. It's something you love."

I sat and thought. And thought. And thought. Fashion? Art? Animals? All options I had considered before casting them aside.

"Think back," said Mario. "Back over the years."

Home. Parents. Mom and Dad splitting up. Jane. Clare. Marcie. The Bridesmaids' Club. That was my best memory—getting that started, collecting all my data, going to the wedding shows, planning weddings with Demi and Maryam. What else? No. Not what else—that was it! The *Bridesmaids'* Club!

"The Bridesmaids' Club. Of course! But could I? Would I be allowed to? It wouldn't be like a job. It would be like all my dreams come true."

"Best sort of job, I'd say," said Mario.

It was like a light had come on in my head. Ping! Obvious. *So* obvious. I got up and hugged Mario.

"This is perfect, *better* than perfect. I've been preparing for this all my life. Wedding planner. *Wedding* planner. That's what I'll do."

*Hallelujah!* I thought as I sat back down. I couldn't wait to tell Demi and Maryam. We could start an agency. With Demi a photographer and Maryam a designer, we would be a perfect team. Nessa had said that what I learned as a Zodiac Girl would last me a lifetime, and it was suddenly all fitting into place, like pieces of a jigsaw puzzle. Marcie's wedding, not mine. Other people's weddings, not mine. I had learned that there were many ways of doing things, many sides to an argument, and that was okay. I wouldn't pressure my clients into what *I* thought was a perfect wedding. Instead, I would help them to create *their own* perfect day. Yea! I had never felt so happy.

"Thank you, Mario. You really are the best career guide I have ever met," I said.

Mario smiled. "You're welcome, although I wouldn't say that I did very much."

"You pointed me in the right direction, and that's what I'll do, too, when I work as a wedding planner. I won't impose my ideas, I'll point people in the direction of what's best for them."

"Sounds good to me," said Mario as I headed for the door.

Now all that was needed was for Sam to win back Marcie, and then I could get on with planning my first wedding—theirs.

# Chapter Fourteen

# For Sam

"I know what I want to be," I announced to Demi and Maryam, who were waiting for me outside the library.

Demi rolled her eyes. "What's this week's career choice?"

"No. This is it. Really it. I feel so happy, I can't tell you," I said. "I mean I *can* tell you, finally. I have decided." I did a little skip and a jump, I felt so good about it.

"Well, what is it?" asked Maryam.

"Wedding planner."

"Wedding planner?" they chorused, and their faces broke into grins. "Wedding planner! Of *course!*"

"Totally, utterly brilliant," said Demi.

"Why didn't we think of it?" asked Maryam. "It was staring us in the face."

"I know," I said. "That's what Mario said, too."

"No doubts, no changing your mind?" asked Demi.

I shook my head. "Nope. I am one hundred percent up for this, and I think it should herald the end of

145

the Bridesmaids' Club—"

Demi and Maryam's faces dropped. "No," gasped Demi. "But—"

"The end of the Bridesmaids' Club and the *beginning* of the Wedding Planners' team," I said. "We'll run our own agency. You. Me. We can do the whole thing . . . Outfits, shoes, locations, photos. Honeymoons, themed ceremonies. Whatever the bride and groom want. Emphasis being on whatever *they* want, and we're talking Velcro, bungee, Bridezilla, even under water. We will offer traditional and alternative."

Maryam clapped her hands. "Yea!" she said.

We put our hands on each other's shoulders and skipped down the hallway together.

I stopped. "And why stop at weddings?" I said. "If being a Zodiac Girl has taught me anything, it's to expect the unexpected. To be flexible. Know what I mean?"

"Yeah," said Demi. "I guess. So?"

"So I think we should think bigger than just wedding planners. Why stop at weddings? That week with Marcie's crazy wedding list really did teach me to push the boundaries. We could plan all sorts of events. Parties . . . You name it! We could do anything because if there's one thing we're good at, it's planning."

"And research," Maryam added.

"We could maybe even get into TV production and movies," said Demi enthusiastically.

"We could. Okay. So we start with our wedding and party agency and see where we go," I said. "We plan, but like we did with Marcie, we go with the flow, too."

I felt ecstatic. The ideas kept coming. Maryam, Demi, and I kept building the fantasy until the agency started to seem real in my imagination.

"In the meantime, we have our first job," I said.

"Ah, yes," said Maryam.

"But, do we?" asked Demi.

I nodded. "Sam and Marcie. But our job isn't to plan their wedding. Our job is to get them back together."

We spent the next few days doing what we did best— planning and research—and since it was my last week as Zodiac Girl, I decided to make the most of it and ask Nessa and her friends to help. Together we found the best fresh flowers flown in every morning from Holland. Joe Joeve told me where he got the most scrumptious, soft-centered chocolates and also gave me a list of the most romantic locations for a cozy candlelit supper. We researched the best music to tug at the heartstrings. We found candles that smelled of tuberose, and aftershave for Sam to wear that was guaranteed to melt the last of Marcie's resistance.

Hermie found a fantastic limo company perfect to take Marcie to the chosen restaurant, and I instructed the chauffeur to treat her like a princess.

Uri provided fun gifts like fluffy teddy bears, balloons that said "I Love You," T-shirts that had "I'm Sorry" written on the front. Hermie found a website that could help you write poems in any style—funny, passionate, apologetic. By the time we were finished, not even a person with a heart of stone would be able to turn Sam down.

I made a list of "ways to win your girlfriend back," and Demi, Maryam, and I went over to Sam's house early on Thursday evening. He opened the door looking pale and stressed, just like Marcie had when she had been over last night.

"You really think this might work?" he asked after he let us into his hallway and we stepped over roller blades and maneuvered our way past his bicycle. I handed him my list, which he glanced over.

"All you can do is try," I said.

"Love favors the brave," said Demi.

"Love never gives up," said Maryam.

"Love conquers all," I said.

Sam smiled. "What are you three? Love experts?"

"We are. We will be. We're going to be wedding and party planners," I explained.

Sam laughed. "Watch out, world."

"Exactly," I said.

"So, this list. Do I do it all at once, or one at a time?" he asked, sounding nervous, but I was glad to see that he was taking it seriously.

"One at a time at first," I said. "And then maybe go for a crescendo-type finale in the restaurant with the violins and candles."

"You could even sing," Demi suggested.

"Right," he said. "Um. Think I'll start with the chocolates."

"Fingers crossed," I said.

"And toes."

He looked so worried and so like a little boy that my heart went out to him. With his mop of blond hair and sky-blue eyes, I could see exactly why Marcie had fallen for him. *He's like the chocolates we were recommending*, I thought, *soft-centered.* I smiled to myself. *This is all good training. I bet tons of couples almost break up pre-wedding. Getting people to make up is going to be part of the job.*

"Funny, isn't it, Sam?" I said. "I followed your list, and now you're following mine."

He nodded. "I think yours might be more sensible," he said. "I never was very good at romance and mushy stuff. See, I grew up with two older brothers. How was I supposed to learn? My defense was to pretend I didn't care, to make fun of it like I did your Bridesmaids' Club. I am sorry, Chloe. That club represented everything I didn't know about and . . . if

I'm honest, I was threatened by it."

"Really?" I asked. I was surprised. Sam had always seemed so confident. Maybe there were two sides to him as well as everything else. I gave him a massive hug to show all was forgiven.

"Aah!" cooed Demi and Maryam, who were looking on.

I pulled away from the hug. "Now it's up to you, Sam," I said. "Romance and a grand gesture, that's what's called for. Something to knock her off her feet. And have no fear, I think you will succeed because Marcie does love you, and love always wins in the end."

Sam smiled happily. "And she loves you, too. Room for both of us?"

"Deffo," I said. "And, oh, I just remembered! You're compatible astrologically. I forgot to mention that. A friend of mine told me at the wedding show. Marcie's a Leo and you're a Sagittarius, both fire signs. A great match."

"Wow! Is there anything you don't know when it comes to romance?" asked Sam.

"Probably, but I am going to make it my business to find out."

Sam grinned and then saluted. "Aye-aye, Captain Chloe. Love Cadet Sam, reporting for duty."

The three of us saluted him back. "Mission Get Back Marcie. Proceed."

# Epilogue

Everything turned out FABulous in the end. Nessa, Hermie, and Uri helped me with my presentation, and not only did I pass with flying colors, I also signed up several clients for graduation parties. My parents and even my sisters Jane and Clare were impressed.

The Hendy wedding got a double-page spread in the local paper, the *Osbury Times*, with eight fabulous photos. The piece read:

**Marcie Bradbury and Sam Hendy were married on Sunday afternoon at a private chapel in Osbury. The bride and her bridesmaids, Chloe, Demi, and Maryam, were beautiful in ivory silk dresses designed by up-and-coming designer Nessa of Celestial Creations. Bouquets of cream roses and ivy accented the wedding party's glamourous attire. The groom was breathtakingly handsome in a white suit.**

**The reception was held at Osbury Hall,**

where the guests feasted on a gourmet meal provided by Joe Joeve of Europa Catering. As the guests were eating, the groom slipped out, later to be seen flying overhead in a small aircraft that looped the loop and wrote "Marcie, I love you" in the sky. Moments later, he was joined by several other small aircraft flown by members of the Celestial Weddings company. The planes let go thousands of white rose petals, which showered down upon the wedding party, filling the air with the smell of roses after a rain. The bride is said to have been "knocked off her feet by the gesture." Later, she praised her husband and her bridesmaids, thanking them for organizing every last detail and making her day everything she had ever hoped for.

After the reception, the party retired to the Osbury Gardens, where a variety of activities had been organized. Guests tried roller-skating and trampolining, and some even dressed up in costumes. It was amusing to see Spiderman sipping champagne with a gorilla and Wonder Woman enjoying canapés with a Viking warrior. Toward the end of the afternoon, the groom tried bungee jumping from a large crane. As he leaped into the air, a banner unfolded behind him. It said, *"Marcie, I've really fallen for you."*

Everyone agreed that it was the most romantic and fun wedding they had ever attended. Sadly, the groom had to be taken to the hospital soon after his jump. He was suffering whiplash but is said to be recovering nicely.

# Are you a typical Libra?

**You go out shopping for a new party dress and you find two you really like. What do you do?**

**A**) Flip a coin—you will never be able to choose.

**B**) Ask your friend for her advice and choose her favorite.

**C**) Buy both. You'll need another one eventually!

**A new girl joins your school and she is wearing shoes that are really unfashionable right now. What do you do?**

**A**) Shrug it off and introduce yourself. Maybe they're so ugly they're actually cool!

**B**) Vow not to be friends with her. There's no excuse for bad shoes.

**C**) Tell her that nobody likes her shoes. Somebody needs to tell her!

**You go to the movies with a group of friends, but none of you can decide what to see. What type of movie would you most enjoy?**

**A**) Horror—something with lots of gruesome monsters to scare you all!

**B**) Romantic comedy—something to make you laugh